GW01464902

STANDARD GRADE
BIOLOGY
REVISION NOTES

Denyse Lukowiecki

Published by   Leckie & Leckie
8 Whitehill Terrace
St Andrews KY16 8RN
Tel 0334 - 75656

A CIP Catalogue record for this book is available
from the British Library.

ISBN 0–9515718–7–7

Leckie & Leckie

CONTENTS

Note

This book covers all the Knowledge and Understanding for General and Credit level at Standard Grade. Your teacher will be able to tell you which parts you need to cover if you are sitting the General level paper only.

1. The Biosphere

Investigating an Ecosystem

The place where an organism (i.e. an animal or plant) lives is called a **habitat**.

If we want to find out as much as possible about a particular habitat, we have to carry out an investigation which involves

1. collecting the organisms; 2. identifying the organisms; 3. measuring the physical conditions.

1. Sampling techniques
Obviously we cannot collect all the organisms within a habitat, so we must take a sample.
Two examples of sampling techniques are:

for animals - a pitfall trap	*for plants - a quadrat*
cup →	The cup is placed in the hole, making sure that the top is level with the ground so that the animals fall in. However, some animals which fall in may be eaten by predators, such as spiders, which also fall in.		The quadrat is a frame divided into squares. It is thrown **randomly** on the area being sampled. The number of squares which contain the plant being studied are counted, **not** the number of plants in each square.

2. Identifying organisms
To identify organisms in a sample a **key** must be used.

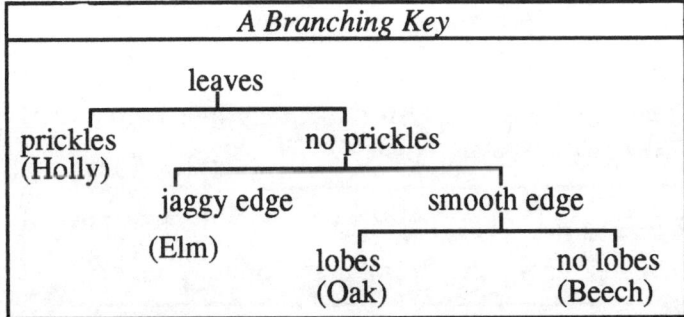

A Branching Key	*A Paired Statement Key*
leaves — prickles (Holly) / no prickles — jaggy edge (Elm) / smooth edge — lobes (Oak) / no lobes (Beech)	1. with prickles .... Holly with no prickles....... 2 2. jaggy edge............. Elm smooth edge .... 3 3. lobes .... Oak no lobes .... Beech

3. Measuring abiotic factors

An **abiotic** factor is a **physical** factor (e.g. **light** or **moisture**) which can affect the organisms living in a particular habitat. Other abiotic factors are **temperature** and **oxygen concentration**.

An abiotic factor can normally be measured using a meter.

measuring light	*measuring moisture*
A light meter is used. To avoid errors, you must be careful not to shade the meter and always hold it the same way when making the reading.	A moisture meter is used. To avoid errors, you must be careful that you place the moisture probe firmly in the ground and wipe it afterwards.

Effect of abiotic factors	Reason why
green plants not found in areas with low light intensity	plants need light for photosynthesis
most land organisms not found in very dry or very wet areas	very dry - they become dehydrated very wet - plant roots are deprived of oxygen

How it works

1. What is an ecosystem?

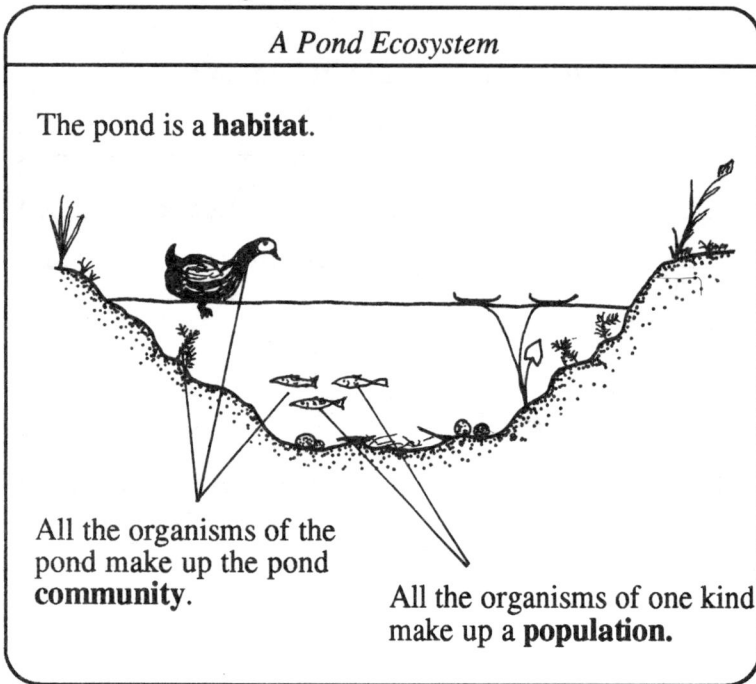

A Pond Ecosystem

The pond is a **habitat**.

All the organisms of the pond make up the pond **community**.

All the organisms of one kind make up a **population.**

The diagram opposite shows all the living and non-living parts that make up a pond ecosystem. All the parts of an ecosystem are inter-related.

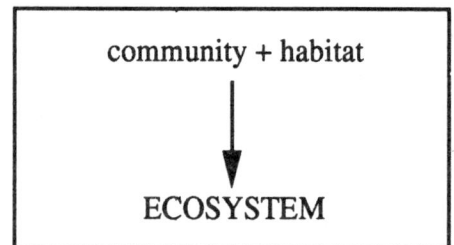

community + habitat

↓

ECOSYSTEM

2. Food and energy in an ecosystem

All living things need energy. They obtain their energy from food. All the energy in an ecosystem comes from the sun, because plants use light energy from the sun to make food.

Plants are called **producers** because they make their own food by a process called **photosynthesis**.

Animals are called **consumers** because they obtain their energy by **eating** plants or other animals.

The way in which energy, in the form of food, passes from plants to animals and then to other animals can be shown by a **food chain**.

grass → field vole → kestrel

| **this is a producer** | **this is a primary consumer** | **this is a secondary consumer** |

The **arrow** in a food chain points from the food to the feeder and shows the **direction of energy flow**.

3. Food webs
A plant or animal usually belongs to several food chains. This connection between food chains forms a food web.

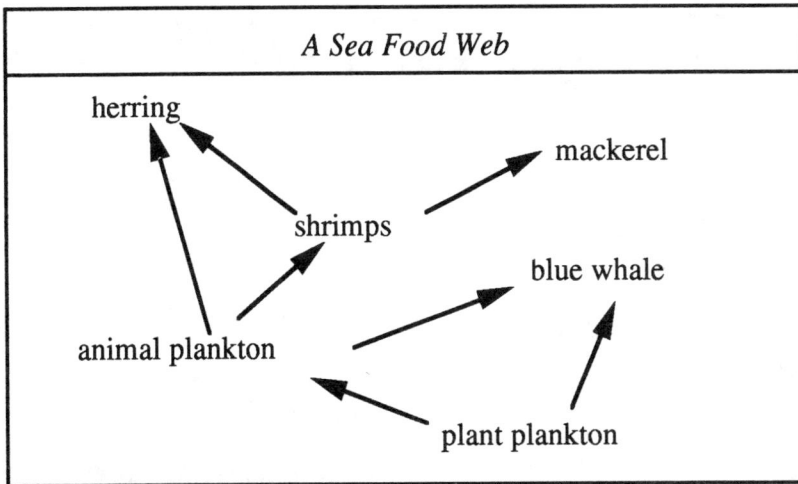

```
            A Sea Food Web
   herring
                        mackerel
         shrimps
                      blue whale
   animal plankton

              plant plankton
```

All food webs are delicately balanced. The removal of one organism can have a serious effect on the food web.

In the sea food web shown opposite, if fishermen catch large numbers of shrimps then the numbers of herring and mackerel will fall because they have less food.

4. Energy loss in a food chain
As energy is passed along a food chain, each organism uses some of it. This means that energy is lost at each stage in a food chain. The ways in which energy is lost are shown below.

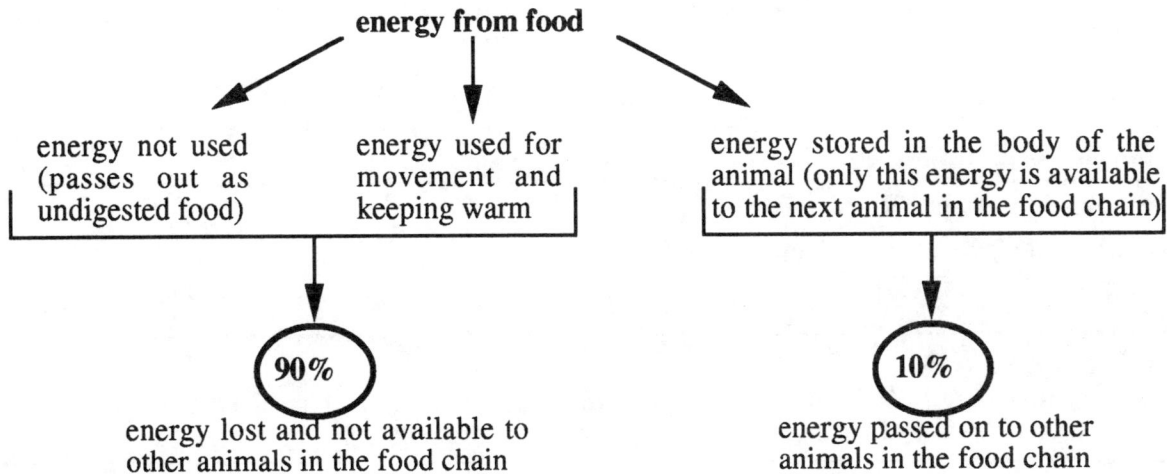

energy from food

energy not used (passes out as undigested food)

energy used for movement and keeping warm

energy stored in the body of the animal (only this energy is available to the next animal in the food chain)

90% energy lost and not available to other animals in the food chain

10% energy passed on to other animals in the food chain

5. Pyramid of numbers
As you move along a food chain, the size of the organism increases but the number of them decreases.

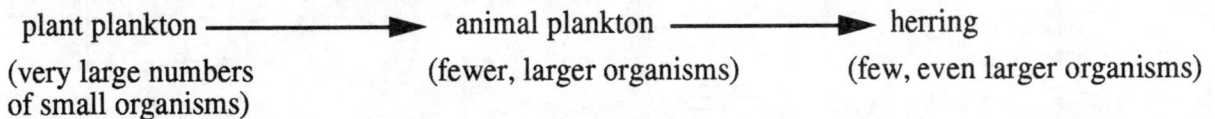

plant plankton ⟶ animal plankton ⟶ herring

(very large numbers of small organisms) (fewer, larger organisms) (few, even larger organisms)

This can be shown by drawing a pyramid.

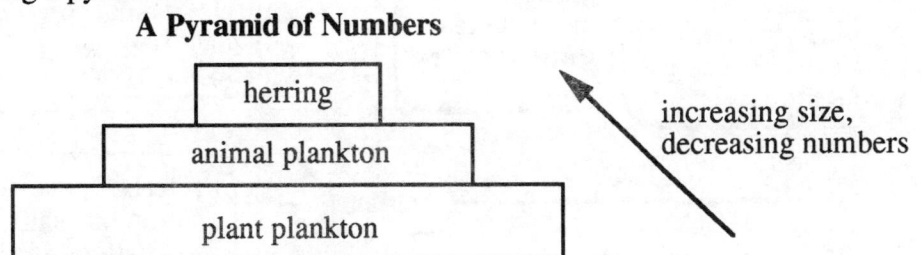

A Pyramid of Numbers

```
        herring
     animal plankton
      plant plankton
```

increasing size, decreasing numbers

A more accurate idea of the quantity of animal and plant material in a food chain is obtained by constructing **a pyramid of biomass**. This represents the mass of all the organisms at each level and gives a much better representation of actual quantity of animal and plant material at each level.

6. Population growth

The size of most populations tends to stay roughly the same. The size of a population stays the same as long as the birth rate is the same as the death rate.

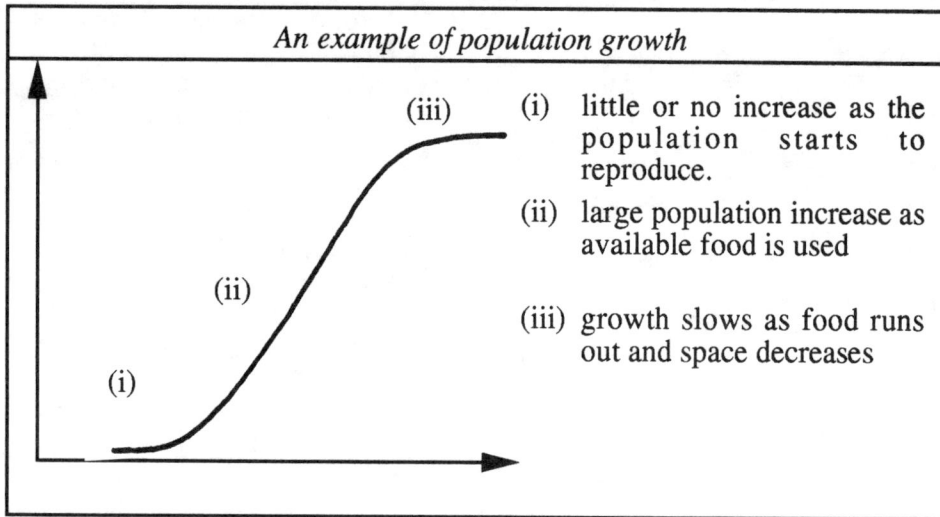

An example of population growth

(i) little or no increase as the population starts to reproduce.

(ii) large population increase as available food is used

(iii) growth slows as food runs out and space decreases

In most populations there is a check on numbers which prevents a population explosion. Populations can be checked by:

(a) predators

(b) disease

(c) limited food supply

(d) lack of space which may prevent breeding.

7. Competition

If different organisms both eat the same food then competition will occur. Plants compete for light and water. Animals compete for food and a place to live. When competition occurs, some organisms will be more successful than others. These organisms will be more likely to survive.

8. Nutrient cycles

Bacteria and fungi are very important to animals and plants. They feed on dead animals and plants and are known as **decomposers**.

Decomposers are important because:

(a) they get rid of dead animals and plants;

(b) they release chemicals from dead organisms which go into the soil and help keep it fertile.

9. The nitrogen cycle

All living things need **nitrogen** to make **protein**. Plants obtain nitrogen from the soil by taking in nitrates. Animals obtain nitrogen by eating plants or other animals.

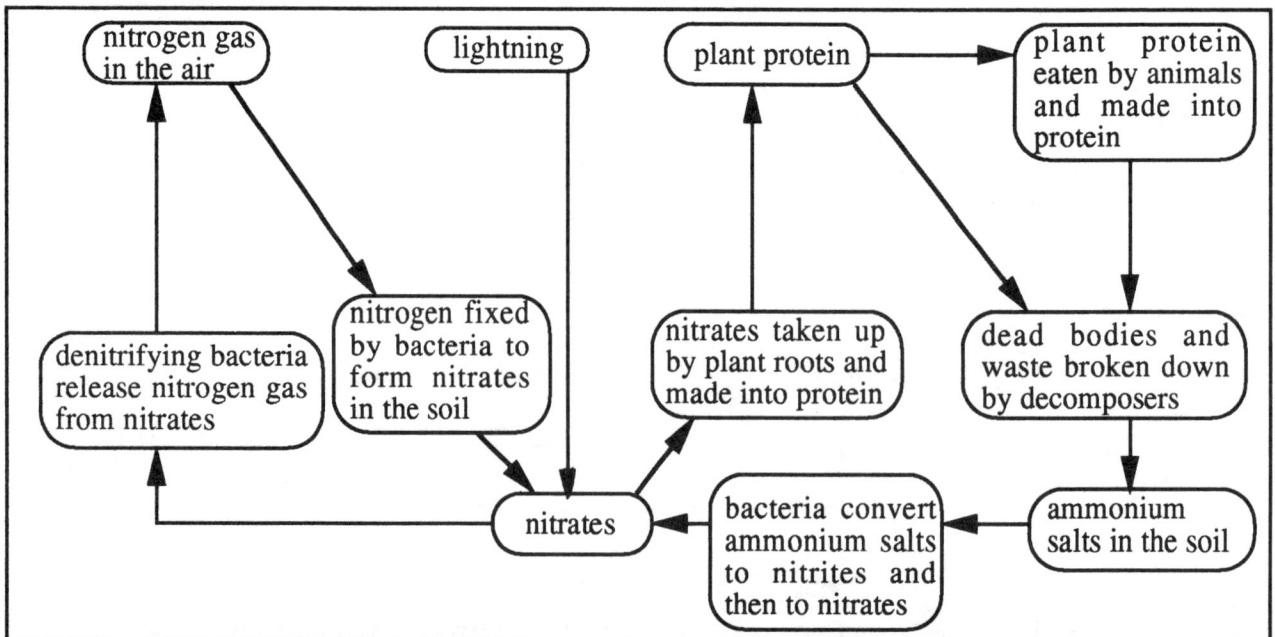

Nitrogen fixing means **absorbing nitrogen gas** from the atmosphere to make **nitrates**. Some bacteria in the soil can do this. Also, some plants (e.g. peas and clover) have swellings on their roots in which these types of bacteria live.

6

Control and Management

1. Sources of pollution

Pollution is caused by the presence of a substance that is harmful to an animal or plant (e.g. oil in the sea). Pollutants come from three main sources - industry, agriculture and domestic. They can affect air, fresh water, sea and land. Here are some examples:

Source of pollution	Substance which causes pollution	Effect of pollutant
industry	sulphur dioxide	causes acid rain
agriculture	pesticides	can be washed into rivers and damage habitats and organisms
domestic	car exhaust fumes	the lead in car exhausts can cause brain damage in young children

2. Controlling pollution

It is essential that the activities of people are controlled so that pollution is reduced, for example:

Pollutant	Method of control
soot in smoke	Clean Air Acts prohibit factories from releasing black smoke
lead in exhaust fumes	introduction of unleaded petrol
domestic sewage	treatment at sewage works before waste is discharged

3. Sewage and pollution

Sewage is a common pollutant. Waste like this is called **organic waste** and can cause many changes in the water. Organic waste provides food for bacteria and allows them to grow and reproduce. When bacteria feed on the sewage, they use up the oxygen in the water. This means that there is less oxygen for other organisms such as fish and insects.

The chart below shows the changes that take place in a stretch of river polluted by sewage.

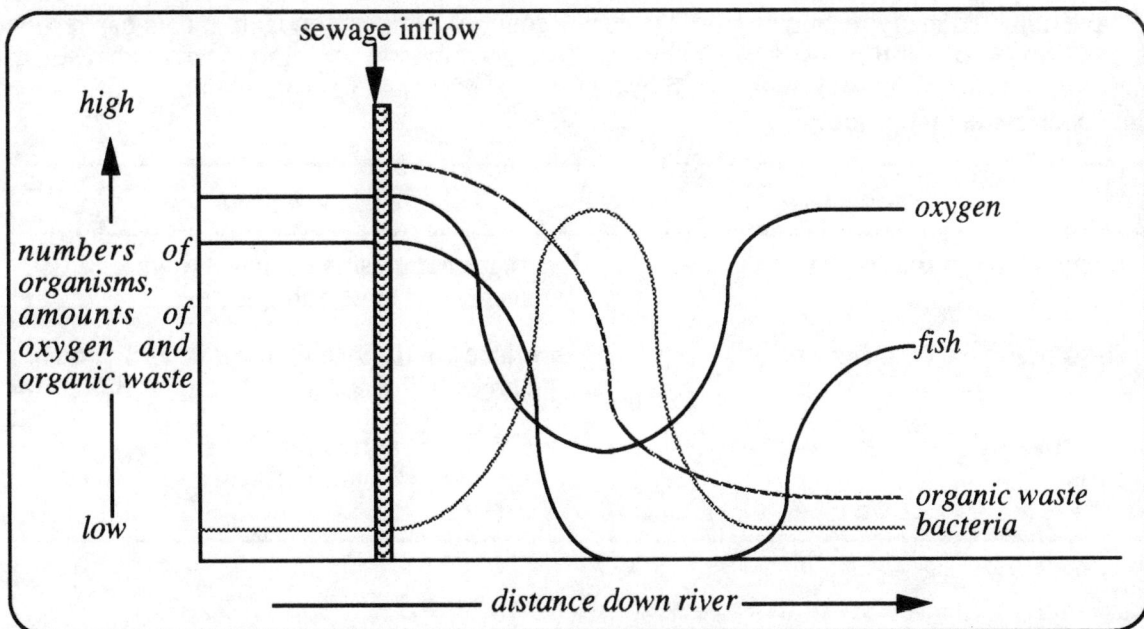

As the level of sewage pollution rises, the level of bacteria rises because the bacteria feed off the sewage which provides energy for growth and reproduction.

At the same time, the level of oxygen falls because the bacteria use up the oxygen as they break down the organic waste in the sewage.

Another effect is that animals, such as fish, stonefly nymphs and shrimps, decrease in numbers.

4. Pollution indicators

Some animals are only able to live in water which contains a lot of oxygen. Other animals can survive in water that contains little or no oxygen. The presence or absence of particular organisms can indicate whether the water is polluted or not. These animals are called **indicator species**.

Animals found in water with low levels of oxygen	sludge worm	rat-tailed maggot	blood worm
Animals found in water with high levels of oxygen	mayfly nymph	stone fly nymph	shrimp

5. Energy sources and pollution

Most of our energy comes from power stations which burn **fossil fuels** (coal, oil and gas).

This results in harmful gases, such as sulphur dioxide and nitrogen dioxide, being released into the air. When these gases dissolve in rain water they form acid rain.

Some alternatives to fossil fuels as sources of energy are:

(a)   solar power (using the sun's light energy);

(b)   wind power (using the movement energy from wind);

(c)   tidal power (using the movement energy of tides);

(d)   nuclear power is also an alternative but it can be dangerous because it produces toxic waste which is difficult to get rid of.

6. Management of resources

People have obtained many resources from the earth (coal, oil, timber, food, etc). This has resulted in the destruction or disruption of many habitats. Conservation is very important because many resources will not last forever or may run short. Three examples of poor management of resources and some possible solutions are:

Poor management	*Possible solution*
overfishing in the North Sea	increase net mesh size to allow smaller fish to survive or have fish quotas.
destruction of rain forests	produce food more efficiently and control the areas being cut down for agriculture.
overuse of land leading to desert soils	use different agricultural practices (crop rotation, natural fertilisers).

2. The World of Plants

Introducing Plants

The **sun** is the **source of all energy** on earth. Plants are the link between the sun and other living things. Without green plants practically all life on earth would not exist. People rely on there being a wide variety of plants yet plant habitats are under constant threat.

1. The importance of plants

Plants are required:

(a)   for plant breeding to produce new varieties;

(b)   as habitats for other organisms;

(c)   as the initial source of food in a food web;

(d)   for gas balance in the atmosphere;

(e)   for raw materials, food and medicines;

(f)   for improving our surroundings.

2. The uses of plants

The range of use of plants is enormous. They can be used for food, raw materials in industry and also for medicines. Here are some examples:

Foods	Raw materials	Medicines
- wheat for bread - palms for oil - sugar cane for sugar - grapes for wine	- jute plant for string - flax plant for linen - rose petals for perfume - heather for dyes	- foxglove plants for digitalis (a muscle relaxant) - poppy for morphine - cinchona tree for quinine

3. The effect of reducing plant species

Plants, especially trees, are essential for maintaining life on this planet. However, certain activities are having quite serious effects on the environment. The destruction of habitats (such as the rain forests) means that many plant species are being lost. Other examples are:

(a)   destruction of the eucalyptus trees in Australia has resulted in a decrease in koalas because this tree is their main food source;

(b)   selective breeding has resulted in a loss of certain plant species.

4. The potential uses of plants

Some new techniques have allowed scientists to use plants to produce new products or to grow greater numbers of the plant, for example:

(a)   the extraction of protein (mycoprotein) from a fungus which can then be used as a food;

(b)   the growing (culture) of oil palm cells to produce large numbers of individual plants from which palm oil can be extracted.

Scientists are always looking for plants that they can use to produce new products. There are still many species of plants which have not yet been discovered and may have a potential use. The destruction of habitats, however, means that some of these plants may be lost forever.

The potential of different vegetable oils, as possible sources of fuel, is one new use of plants being investigated. However, investigations like this can take a very long time and can also be expensive.

Growing Plants

In order to reproduce, plants produce seeds. This involves a number of stages in the plant life cycle.

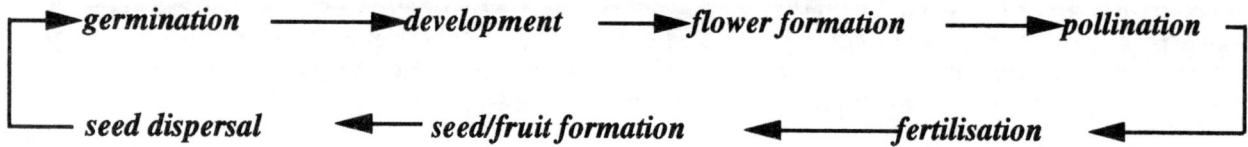

germination ⟶ development ⟶ flower formation ⟶ pollination

seed dispersal ⟵ seed/fruit formation ⟵ fertilisation ⟵

1. Structure of a seed and germination

Germination is the stages involved in the development of a new plant from the embryo plant in the seed.

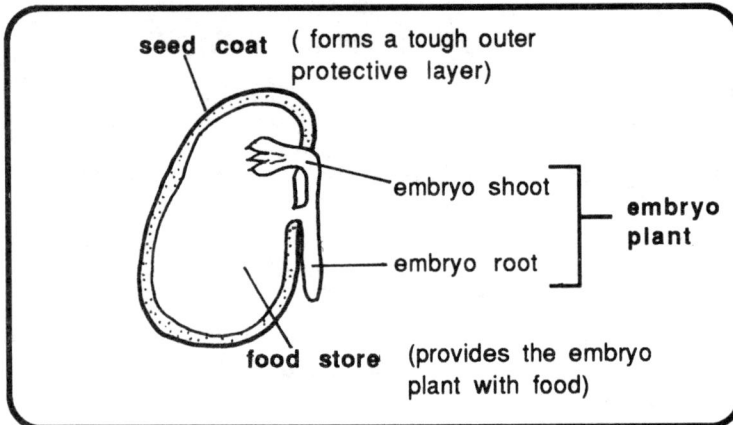

water	needed by the seed for enzymes to digest stored food
oxygen	needed to produce energy for germination
heat	needed for the enzymes involved in germination to work

At very high (above 45°C) and very low (0° to 5°C) temperatures seed germination is very low or zero. Seeds normally have a high percentage germination over a range of temperatures (18° to 25°C), with highest germination rate at a temperature known as the optimum.

2. Structure of a flower

When a plant is ready to reproduce, it produces flowers. A plant's sex organs are in its flowers.

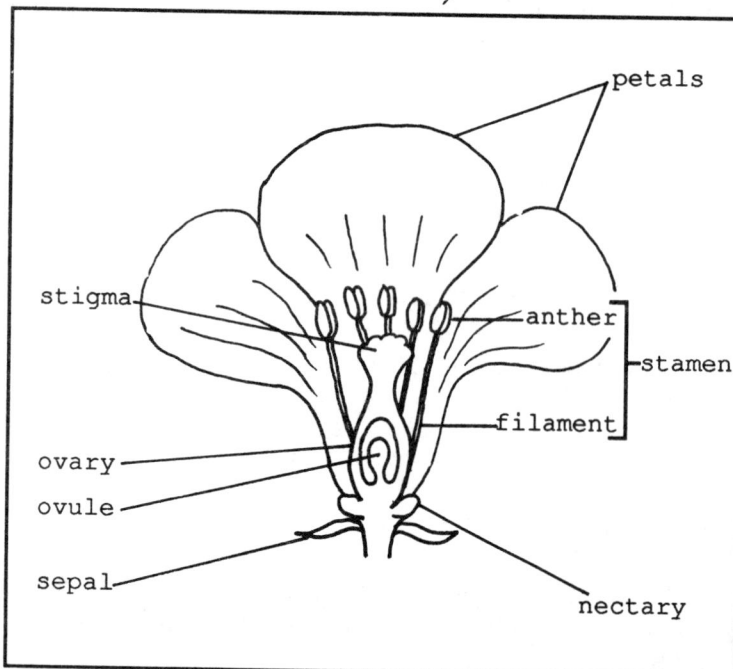

structure	function
sepal	protects the flower bud
petal	attracts insects
stamen	male part of the flower
anther	produces pollen grains
stigma	catches pollen grains
ovary	contains the ovules
nectary	produces nectar, a sugary liquid that attracts insects

10

3. Pollination

A new seed will be formed when the male sex cell in a pollen grain joins up with a female sex cell. Sex cells are called **gametes**.

Pollination involves the **transfer of pollen** from the anther to the stigma.

Pollination can be carried out either by insects or by the wind.

	insect pollinated flowers	*wind pollinated flowers*
petals	brightly coloured and scented to attract insects	green and dull petals, as they do not need to attract insects
pollen	pollen is sticky or spiky to stick to insects' fur	large amounts of very light pollen that will be carried by the wind
stigmas	sticky so that when insects brush past the pollen sticks	feathery stigmas hang outside the flower so that pollen can be trapped on them
stamens	inside the flower so that insects will brush past them and pick up pollen	large and dangle outside to catch the wind which will blow away the pollen
nectar	sticky sweet substance that attracts insects	none produced as they do not need to attract insects

4. Fertilisation

Once the pollen grain has landed on the stigma, the next stage is fertilisation.

Fertilisation involves the fusion of the male gamete and the female gamete.

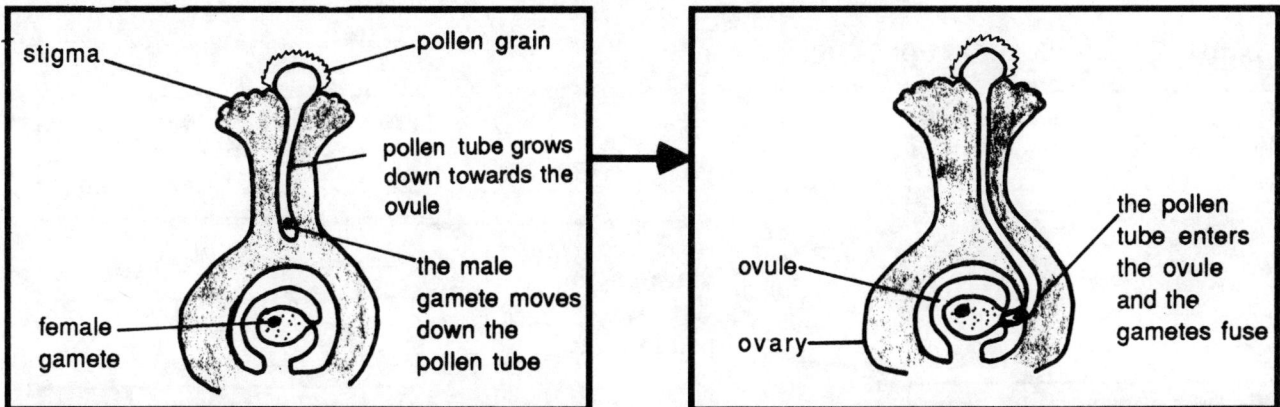

Once fertilisation has taken place, the ovule becomes the seed and the ovary becomes a fruit. The petals then die and drop off.

11

5. Fruit and seed dispersal

A fruit is any part of a plant that contains seeds. There are two kinds of fruit:

(a) Fleshy fruits (e.g. tomato, plum, apple). Here the main part of the fruit is soft and juicy.

(b) Dry fruits (e.g. dandelion, sycamore) Here the main part of the fruit is hard and dry.

Fruit and seeds must be carried away from the parent plant because they would be too crowded and competition would take place for water, light and food.

Fruits and seeds can be dispersed in three ways.

dispersal method	description of some examples	seeds/fruits
wind	- may have extensions which act as parachutes or wings to carry the seed in the wind (e.g. dandelion and sycamore) - fruits may also be shaken like a pepper pot (e.g. poppy)	
animal (external)	- carried away by animals and dropped (e.g. hazelnuts) - have hooks which attach to the animals fur and may be rubbed off later (e.g. burdock)	
animal (internal)	- brightly coloured to attract animals and when eaten the seed survives digestive juices and is passed out in the faeces (e.g. cherry, tomato)	

6. Asexual reproduction

Sexual reproduction involves two parents. Many flowering plants can reproduce in a way that only involves one parent. Some plants grow parts that can break off and become new plants. This is called asexual reproduction and does not involve the formation of sex cells.

There are many ways in which plants can reproduce asexually but the three main ways are:

Runners	Tubers	Bulbs
A runner is a side shoot which grows out from the parent. Where it touches the ground a new plant grows. (e.g. strawberry, spider plant)	An underground food store. Food made in the leaves is stored in the tuber and used as an energy source for new growth. (e.g. potato, dahlia)	A bulb has thick fleshy leaves full of stored food which is used for the growth of a new plant the following year. (e.g. daffodils, onions)

7. Advantages of asexual reproduction

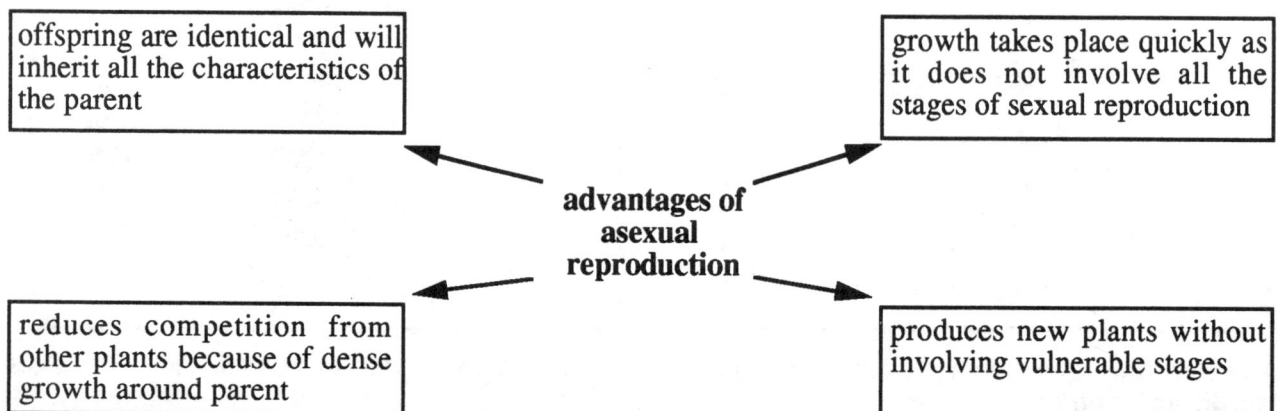

offspring are identical and will inherit all the characteristics of the parent		growth takes place quickly as it does not involve all the stages of sexual reproduction
	advantages of asexual reproduction	
reduces competition from other plants because of dense growth around parent		produces new plants without involving vulnerable stages

12

8. Comparing asexual and sexual reproduction

	Asexual reproduction	*Sexual reproduction*
Advantages	- early quick growth is possible because there are no vulnerable stages involved - offspring will all have the parent plants good characteristics	- variation takes place which may be an advantage if conditions change - allows dispersal of seeds to new areas
Disadvantages	- because there is no variation, weak characteristics can be passed on - competition may be reduced, but overcrowding can take place	- involves many vulnerable stages which the young plant may not survive

> Asexual reproduction involves the formation of **clones**. A clone is a group of cells all originating from the same parent and are all identical to each other and the parent.

9. Artificial propagation

Gardeners make use of a plant's ability to reproduce asexually by using different methods of propagation. Instead of growing seeds, they take a small section of stem, root or leaf. Under the right conditions, these will grow into a whole plant.

Three common methods of propagation are:

Cuttings	*Grafting*	*Layering*
Cuttings are small pieces of stem cut from a healthy plant. The cut stem can be placed in a rooting medium to encourage root growth. (e.g. house plants)	A portion of a plant with good flower or fruit growth is taken and joined to a plant with an established strong root system. (e.g. roses and fruit bushes)	The stem of the parent plant is bent until it touches the ground. It is then held in place until roots have formed. (e.g. carnations)

10. Commercial advantages of artificial propagation

The ability of plants to carry out asexual reproduction has brought enormous benefits in both agriculture and horticulture.

(a) It is a quick method of producing large numbers of new plants, especially by cuttings.

(b) Particular varieties that are required can be produced easily.

(c) Techniques like grafting produce a plant that will grow fruit or flowers of a known variety or quality.

Making Food

1. How plants make food

> Plants make food by a process called **photosynthesis**.

Plants use light energy to make food from carbon dioxide and water. The chemical chlorophyll (which gives plants their green colour) traps the light energy from the sun. This light energy is then converted to chemical energy in the form of glucose. All food chains and food webs rely on plants to manufacture food at the start of the food chain.

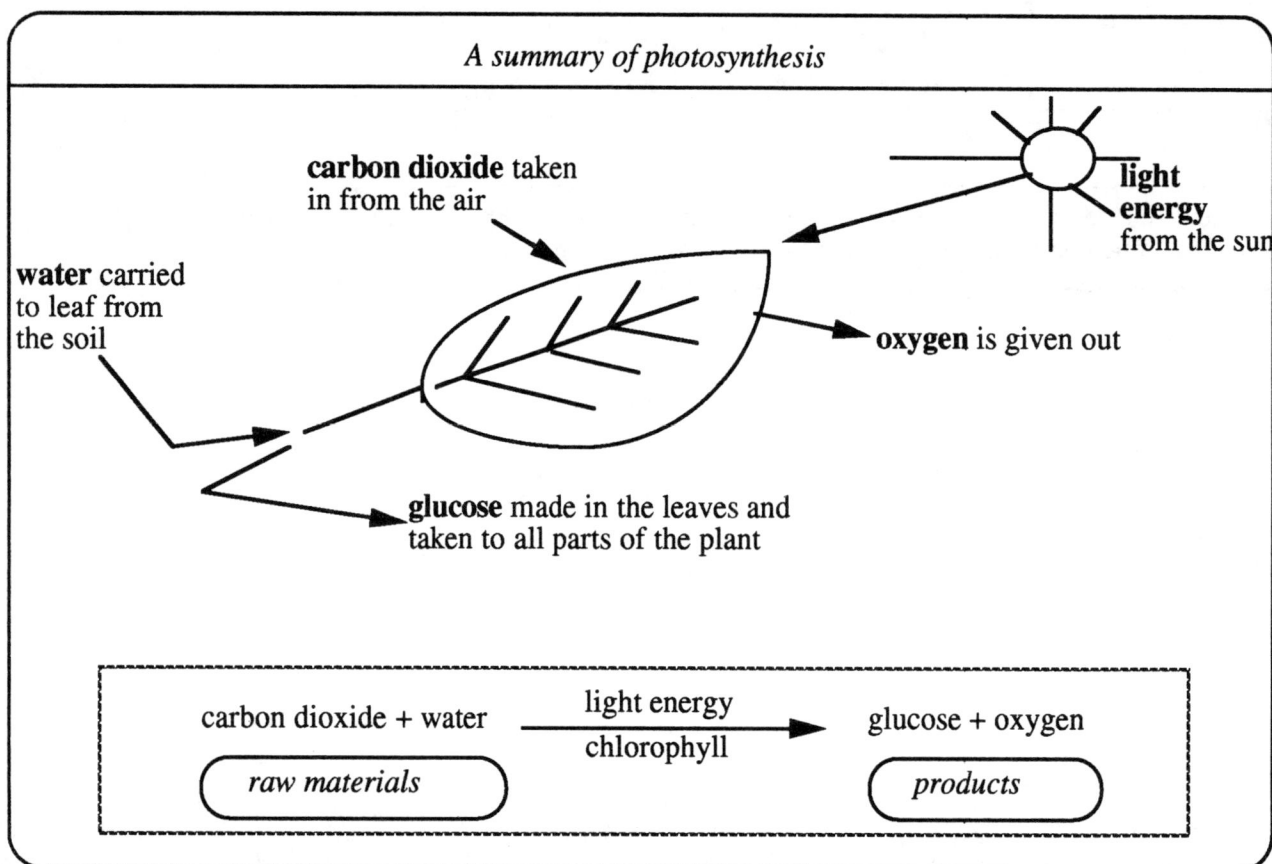

A summary of photosynthesis

carbon dioxide taken in from the air

light energy from the sun

water carried to leaf from the soil

oxygen is given out

glucose made in the leaves and taken to all parts of the plant

$$\text{carbon dioxide} + \text{water} \xrightarrow[\text{chlorophyll}]{\text{light energy}} \text{glucose} + \text{oxygen}$$

raw materials

products

The leaf takes in carbon dioxide through tiny pores on the lower surface of the leaf. One of these pores is called a stoma (plural: stomata). These pores can open or close. Water vapour can be lost from the leaves through the stomata.

2. The use of glucose by plants

The glucose manufactured during photosynthesis is used by the plant in a number of ways.

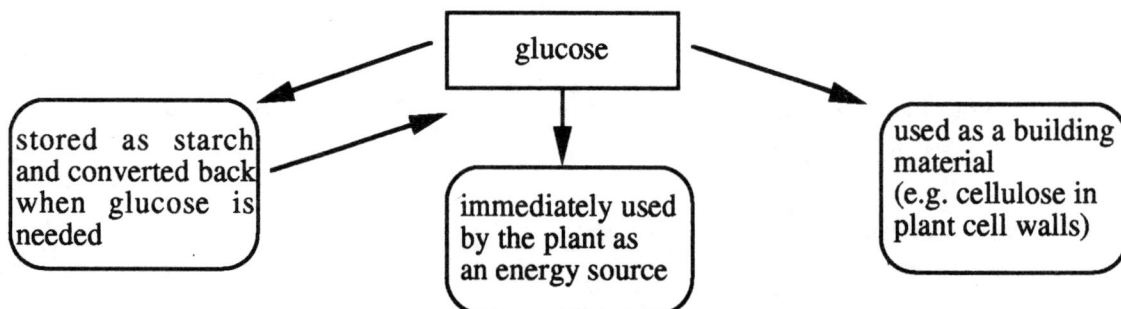

glucose

stored as starch and converted back when glucose is needed

immediately used by the plant as an energy source

used as a building material (e.g. cellulose in plant cell walls)

3. Transport in a plant

Xylem carries water and minerals from the soil to the leaf for photosynthesis.

Phloem carries glucose from the leaves to every part of the plant.

The Structure of Xylem

Xylem cells are dead. The end walls have disintegrated and the side walls have been impregnated with a substance called **lignin**, which strengthens xylem. Xylem also carries minerals and helps support the plant.

lignin

The Structure of Phloem

sieve plate

sieve tube

All phloem cells are alive. The end walls have pores. Food is transported through the pores from cell to cell.

companion cell (provides energy)

4. Structure of a leaf

A leaf has a large surface area and is very thin because:

(a) A large surface allows maximum exposure to sunlight.

(b) A thin leaf means that gases can diffuse quickly to and from the photosynthesising leaf cells.

Internal Structure of a Leaf

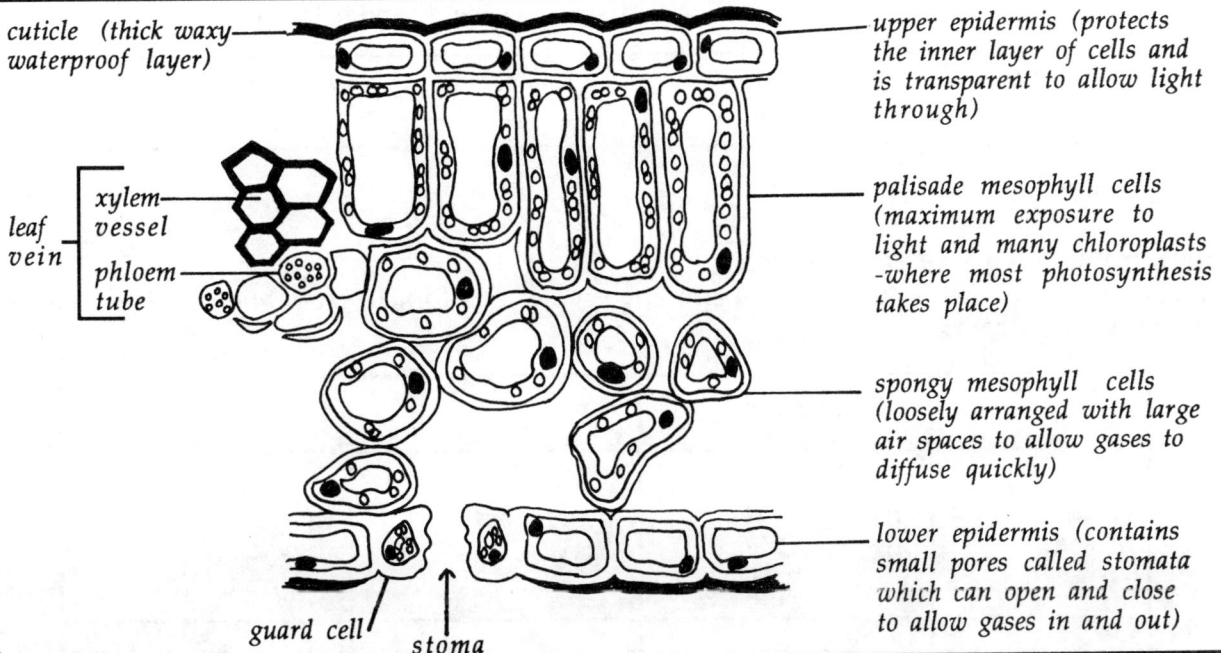

cuticle (thick waxy waterproof layer)

upper epidermis (protects the inner layer of cells and is transparent to allow light through)

leaf vein — xylem vessel — phloem tube

palisade mesophyll cells (maximum exposure to light and many chloroplasts -where most photosynthesis takes place)

spongy mesophyll cells (loosely arranged with large air spaces to allow gases to diffuse quickly)

lower epidermis (contains small pores called stomata which can open and close to allow gases in and out)

guard cell   stoma

5. Limiting factors

Photosynthesis does not only depend on light, carbon dioxide and a suitable temperature, but also on the amounts of each that are available. If they are in short supply, they will cut down or limit the rate of photosynthesis. Light, water, carbon dioxide and temperature can act as limiting factors.

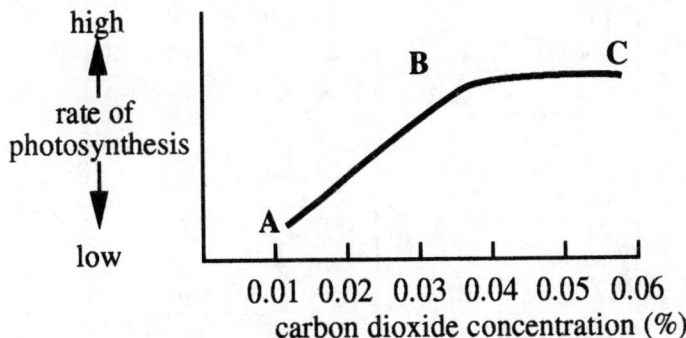

high

↑
rate of photosynthesis
↓

low

A   B   C

0.01 0.02 0.03 0.04 0.05 0.06
carbon dioxide concentration (%)

Carbon dioxide is increased. Temperature and light are kept constant. The limiting factor between A and B is carbon dioxide. The limiting factor between B and C is either light or temperature.

Photosynthesis will only increase if the limiting factor is increased.

3. Animal Survival

The Need for Food

1. Why we need food

All living things need food to survive. There are two ways in which organisms obtain their food:

(a) Plants make their own food by the process of photosynthesis.

(b) Animals rely on ready made food, either by eating plants or other animals.

Any food contains a mixture of chemicals. The main ones are:

Chemical	Function
carbohydrates (e.g. sugar and starch)	provide energy
proteins	needed for growth and repair
fats	provide energy and help insulate the body
vitamins and minerals (e.g. vitamin C and calcium)	needed to stay healthy

2. Chemical structure of food types

Carbohydrates, fats and proteins are mostly large molecules formed from many similar, smaller molecules linked together.

	Carbohydrate	Fat	Protein
elements present	carbon (C) hydrogen (H) oxygen(O)	carbon hydrogen oxygen	carbon hydrogen oxygen nitrogen (N)
basic units they are built from	glucose molecules	fatty acids and glycerol	amino acids
diagram of structure	glucose molecules in a chain	glycerol / fatty acids	amino acids in a chain

3. Breaking down food

The food we eat must be changed before the body can use it. This involves the breakdown of large insoluble food particles into smaller soluble particles that can pass from the small intestine into the bloodstream.

The breakdown of food takes place in two steps:

(a) the **mechanical breakdown** by **teeth**;

(b) the **chemical breakdown** by **enzymes**   e.g. starch $\xrightarrow{\text{enzyme}}$ glucose.

(insoluble) (soluble)

(a) Teeth		
Omnivore (human)	1	incisor - used for biting off food
	2	canine - used for gripping
	3	premolar - used for chewing and grinding
	4	molar - used for chewing and grinding
Carnivore (dog)	1	incisor - used for biting
	2	canine - used for holding and piercing prey
	3	premolar - used for crushing bones
	4	molars - used for crushing bones
	5	carnassial - used for shearing flesh
Herbivore (sheep)	1	incisor - bite against hard pad and shear grass at its roots
	2	gap - no canines present
	3	premolar - used for chewing and grinding
	4	molar - used for chewing and grinding

(b)   The **chemical breakdown** of food takes place in the **gut or alimentary canal**.

The gut is about seven metres long and is coiled round to fit into your body. Most of the coils are in your abdomen. Each part of the gut has a different job to do. The movement of food from the mouth to the anus is slow and may take up to two days.

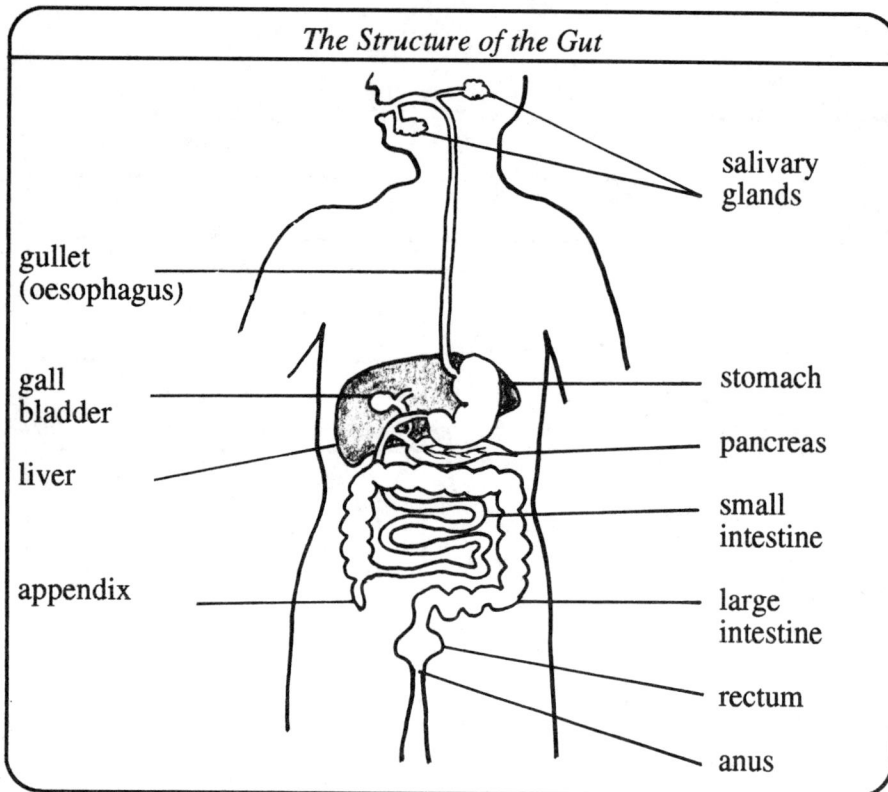

The Structure of the Gut

gullet (oesophagus)

gall bladder

liver

appendix

salivary glands

stomach

pancreas

small intestine

large intestine

rectum

anus

Organs which produce digestive juices

salivary glands
stomach
pancreas
liver
small intestine

4. Moving food along the gut

Food cannot move along the gut by itself - it has to be pushed. This is done by muscles in the gut wall. When food moves along the gut, muscles in the wall contract behind the food and relax in front of it. This pushes the food along the gut. This action by the muscles is called **peristalsis**.

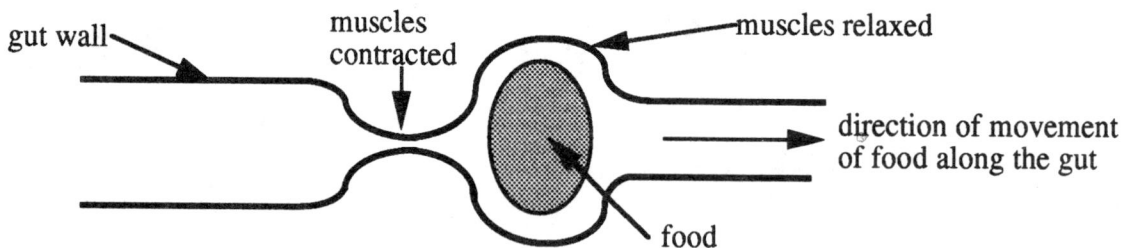

gut wall

muscles contracted

muscles relaxed

direction of movement of food along the gut

food

5. How food is digested

As food passes along the gut, digestive juices are produced by the different organs it passes through. These digestive juices contain enzymes which digest (break down) the carbohydrates, fats and proteins in the food you eat.

In the mouth

Food is chewed into small pieces. Some starch (a carbohydrate) is digested by an enzyme in saliva.

In the stomach

Contractions of the muscles in the stomach wall help to mix food with an enzyme and acid produced by the stomach wall. The acid kills germs and helps the enzyme to work.

18

In the small intestine

All digestion is completed by more enzymes produced by the small intestine and the pancreas.
Food is now in a form the body can use and it is absorbed through the wall of the intestine into the bloodstream, which carries it to the liver.

The small intestine is able to carry out this job efficiently because:-

    (a)   it is long and folded to create a bigger surface;
    (b)   the surface is increased by tiny finger-like projections called villi;

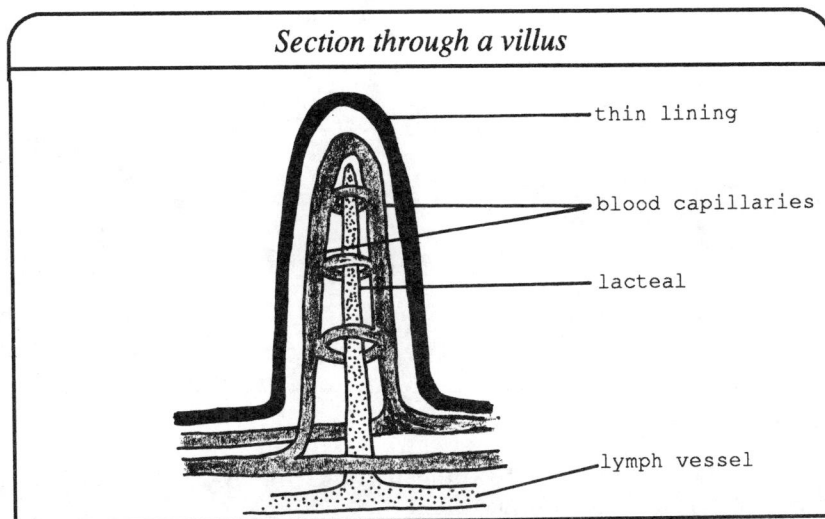

Section through a villus

thin lining
blood capillaries
lacteal
lymph vessel

    (c)   the wall is very thin to allow digested food through quickly and easily;

    (d)   the wall has a good blood supply to carry the digested food away

        -    glucose and amino acids pass into the bloodstream;

        -    fatty acids and glycerol pass into the lacteal.

In the large intestine

What passes into the large intestine is a very watery mash, because it still contains a lot of water. Most of this water is absorbed back into the blood and the undigested remains (faeces) are stored in the rectum and eventually pass out through the anus.

6. Digestive enzymes

Digestive enzymes change the food you eat by breaking down the large, insoluble food molecules into smaller soluble food molecules that can easily be absorbed into the bloodstream.
Each type of food needs a different enzyme to break it down.

enzyme group	substrate	product	example of enzyme in this group and organ it is produced by
amylase	starch	glucose	salivary amylase - salivary glands
protease	protein	amino acids	pepsin - stomach
lipase	fats and oils	fatty acids & glycerol	pancreatic lipase - pancreas

Reproduction in Animals

1. Types of reproduction

There are two ways reproduction can take place:

(a) **Asexual reproduction:** There is only one parent. It does not involve the formation and fusion of sex cells. e.g. *Amoeba*, sea anemone.

(b) **Sexual reproduction:** This type of reproduction involves two parents. The parents have sex organs which produce sex cells. The sex cells are called gametes. The male gametes are sperm, the female gametes are eggs.

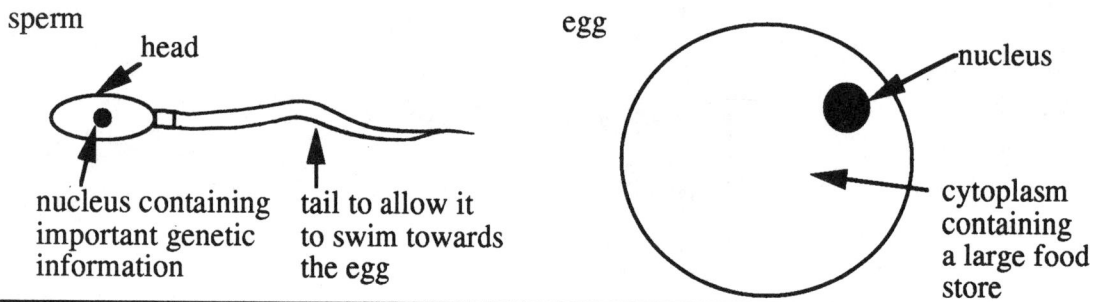

sperm

head

nucleus containing important genetic information

tail to allow it to swim towards the egg

egg

nucleus

cytoplasm containing a large food store

2. Fertilisation and development

For sexual reproduction to take place a sperm nucleus must fuse with an egg nucleus. This is called fertilisation. There are two types of fertilisation:

(a) **External fertilisation** - the eggs are released from the body into the external surroundings and the male then sheds his sperm over the eggs (e.g. fish).

(b) **Internal fertilisation** - the eggs are fertilised by the sperm inside the female's body (e.g. mammals). This is important to land-living animals, as there is no water outside the body to carry the sperm to the egg.

3. Human reproduction

Human reproduction begins with sexual intercourse. During sexual intercourse millions of sperm are passed into the woman's vagina. The sperm then swim up through the womb and into the oviduct. The sperm are attracted to chemicals produced by the egg which has been released into the oviduct.

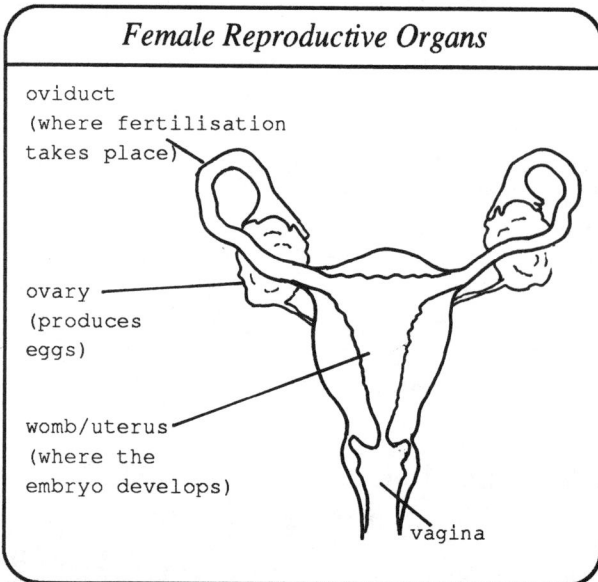

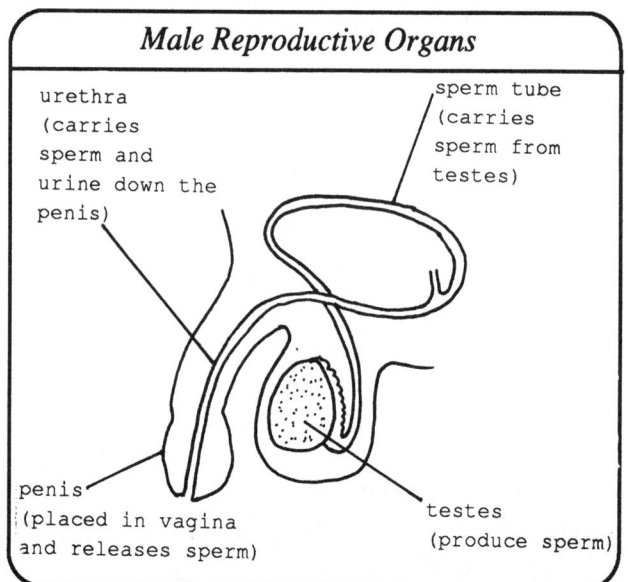

Female Reproductive Organs

oviduct (where fertilisation takes place)

ovary (produces eggs)

womb/uterus (where the embryo develops)

vagina

Male Reproductive Organs

urethra (carries sperm and urine down the penis)

sperm tube (carries sperm from testes)

penis (placed in vagina and releases sperm)

testes (produce sperm)

4. Human development

When the sperm meet an egg, they group round it and the head of one sperm will enter the egg. The nucleus of the sperm and the egg join together. The membrane round the egg then stops any other sperm from entering. The fertilised egg now continues down the oviduct to the womb, dividing many times. The ball of cells, the embryo, attaches itself to the wall of the womb and begins to develop.

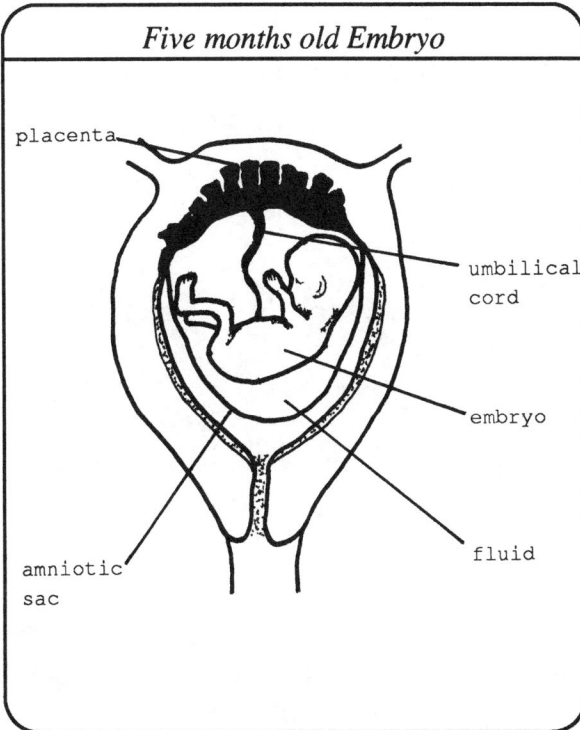

Five months old Embryo

The embryo develops in a bag-like structure called the amniotic sac. This is filled with fluid which helps to protect the embryo as it grows. The fluid cushions it against any bumps or knocks.

The growing embryo is attached to the womb wall by the umbilical cord. The umbilical cord passes into the placenta which is attached to the wall of the womb. The umbilical cord carries carbon dioxide and waste from the baby to the placenta and oxygen and food to the baby.

The mother's blood does not mix with that of the baby's, but the blood vessels are very close and materials can pass easily from the mother to the baby and vice versa. Harmful substances (such as nicotine, alcohol and drugs) can also pass into the baby's blood system and cause harm.

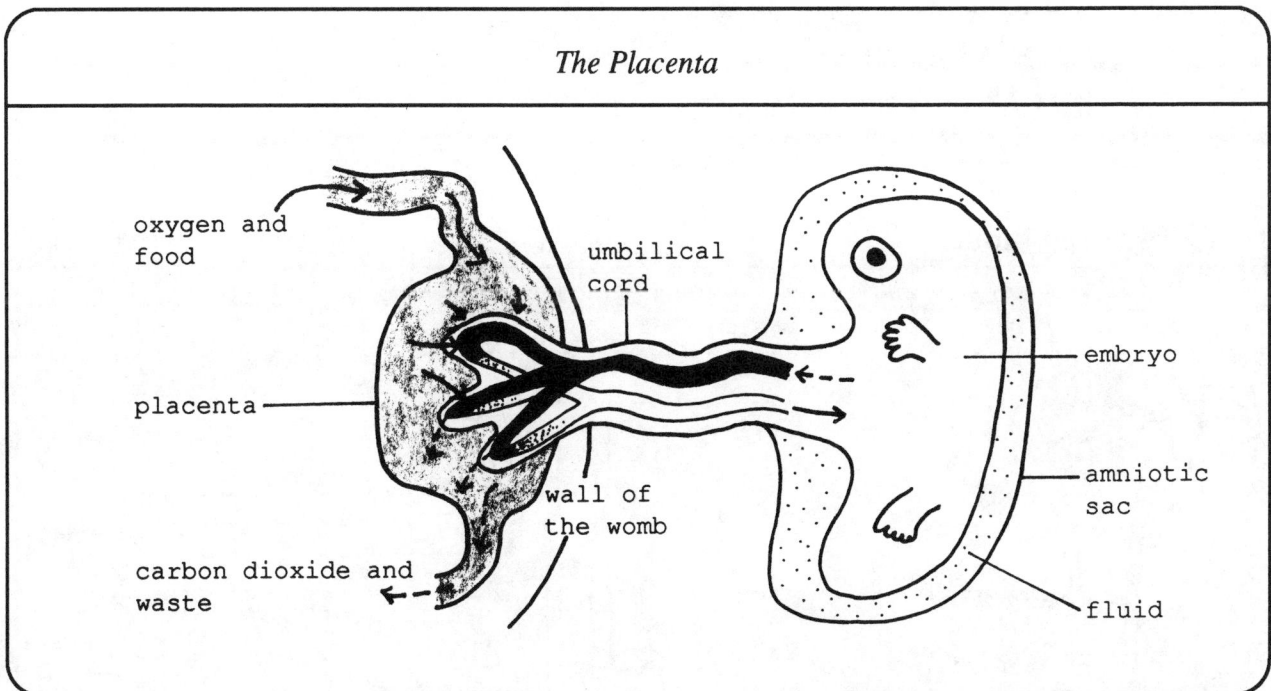

The Placenta

After birth, the young of mammals are very dependent on the adult for care and protection. This is unlike many other animals where the adults have nothing more to do with development after the eggs or sperm are laid (e.g. the frog or trout)

5. Trout development

Trouts' eggs and sperm are shed into water. This stops the eggs from drying out and also allows the sperm to swim to the eggs.

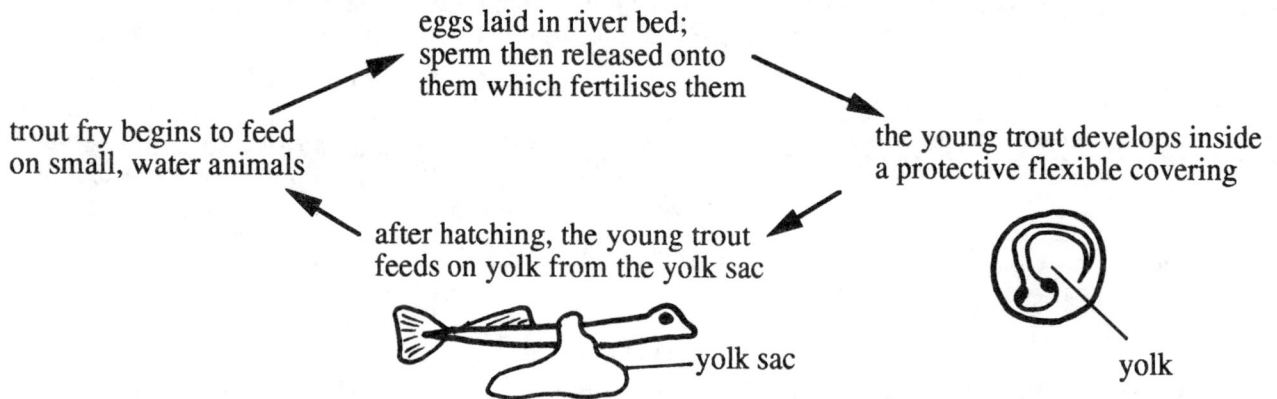

eggs laid in river bed; sperm then released onto them which fertilises them

trout fry begins to feed on small, water animals

the young trout develops inside a protective flexible covering

after hatching, the young trout feeds on yolk from the yolk sac

yolk sac

yolk

6. Egg numbers and survival chances

Many sex cells and young are destroyed during the various stages of development by, for example:

(a)   eggs not being fertlised;   (b)   eggs being eaten;   (c)   eggs being diseased.

The greater the risks involved in the type of reproduction, the greater the number of eggs produced.

animal	number of eggs produced
herring	5,000,000
turtle	100

As the survival chances of the herring are very low (because fertilisation and development are external), the herring produces very large numbers of eggs to compensate and ensure that at least a small proportion will survive and become adults.

Water and Waste

The kidneys are important because they help to get rid of poisonous waste and regulate the amount of water in the body.

1. Structure of the kidneys

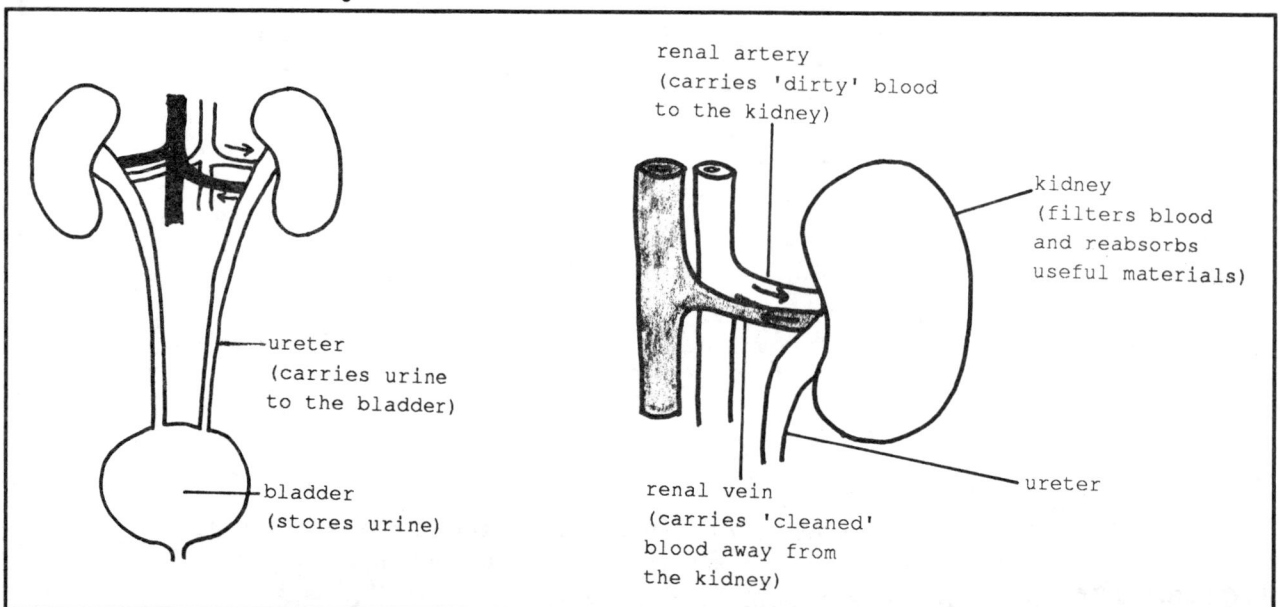

renal artery
(carries 'dirty' blood to the kidney)

kidney
(filters blood and reabsorbs useful materials)

ureter
(carries urine to the bladder)

bladder
(stores urine)

renal vein
(carries 'cleaned' blood away from the kidney)

ureter

2. The kidneys and water balance

Our bodies are 60% water. Too much or too little water is dangerous. You can gain water or lose water in different ways, but the amount of water we gain must be equal to the amount of water we lose. This is called **water balance**. The kidneys help to maintain this balance by producing more or less urine depending on the body's intake.

How water enters and leaves the body			
daily water gain	*cm³*	*daily water loss*	*cm³*
food and drink	1400	urine	700
water made in respiration (when energy is released from food)	350	sweat	500
		breathing	400
		faeces (solid waste)	150
TOTAL	1750	TOTAL	1750

3. The kidneys and waste

As well as being involved in water balance, the kidneys are also involved in getting rid of the poisonous waste substance called **urea**. Urea is produced in the liver.

The kidneys clean blood by filtering it. All your blood is filtered by the kidneys about 300 times a day. The filtering is carried out by millions of tiny little tubes called **nephrons**.

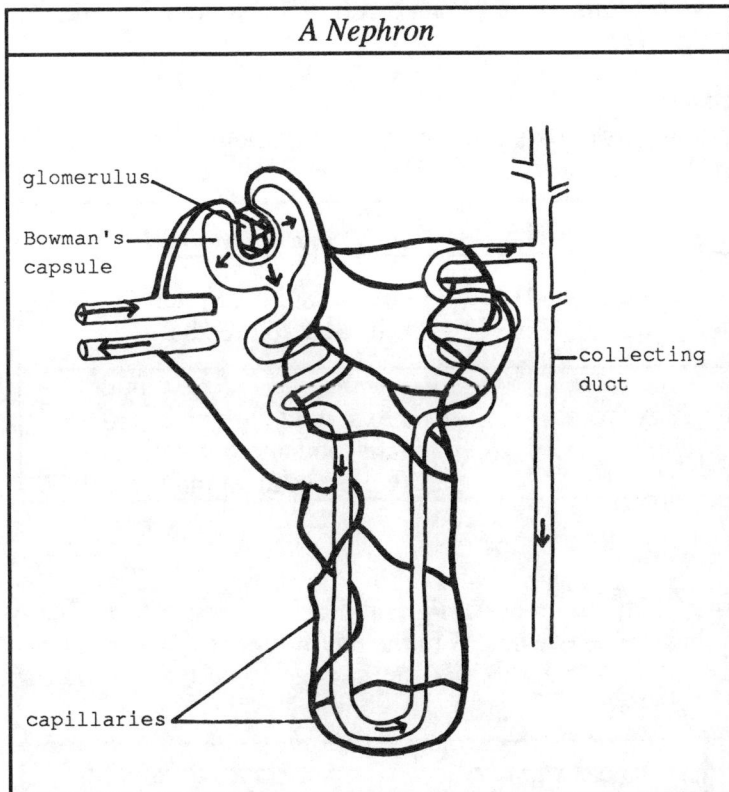

A Nephron

glomerulus
Bowman's capsule
collecting duct
capillaries

Blood enters the nephron along a branch of the renal artery carrying useful substances as well as urea. The renal artery then divides into a group of capillaries called the glomerulus. The glomerulus sits in a cup shape called the Bowman's capsule. Blood is filtered through the glomerulus and Bowman's capsule and into the rest of the nephron. As the liquid passes along the nephron useful substances (like glucose and vitamins) are reabsorbed back into the blood, which passes out of the kidney along the renal vein.

The liquid left in the nephron contains urea, water and other unwanted substances. This liquid now passes into the collecting duct, which empties into the ureter. The ureter drains into the bladder which stores urine until it leaves the body.

4. How urea is produced

During digestion, proteins in our food are broken down by enzymes into amino acids. These amino acids are carried to the liver to be built into new proteins. Any extra amino acids not used are broken down by the liver into urea. The urea is then taken to the kidneys where it is removed in the urine.

5. Control of water balance

No matter how much water the body gains or loses, the kidneys adjust the amount of urine produced to help maintain water balance. This process is controlled by a chemical produced in the brain called **anti-diuretic hormone** (ADH).

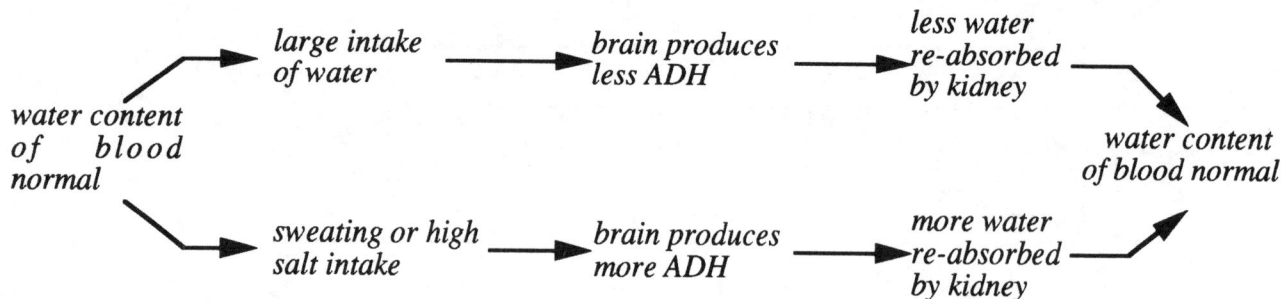

water content of blood normal → large intake of water → brain produces less ADH → less water re-absorbed by kidney → water content of blood normal

water content of blood normal → sweating or high salt intake → brain produces more ADH → more water re-absorbed by kidney → water content of blood normal

6. Kidney damage

If the kidneys stop working because of disease or damage, then the person will die. Kidney failure can be treated by using kidney machines or by kidney transplants.

Kidney machines are very expensive and involve the patient spending a lot of time connected to them.

Kidney transplants are not frequent because of a shortage of donors. The transplanted kidney can also be rejected by the body of the patient.

Responding to the Environment

Living things are found on land, in the air and in water. These surroundings are their environment. An environment has many places, called habitats, where animals or plants can live. Each organism has its own habitat. This has the conditions which they prefer.

1. Responses to changes in their environment

The way in which an animal responds to a stimulus from its surroundings is important to the animal's survival. The conditions an animal chooses are the best for its survival.

animal	stimulus	response	importance to animal
woodlouse	moisture	moves towards moisture	needs to keep breathing system moist to be able to breathe
blowfly maggots	light	moves away from light	need to stay in dark places to obtain food and protection (e.g. in dead animals)

2. Rhythmical behaviour

Some environmental conditions change regularly (e.g. hours of daylight and daily temperatures). Many animals change their behaviour in response to these regular changes in the environment. These changes are examples of rhythmical behaviour. The stimulus that sets off the change is called a **trigger stimulus**.

animal	rhythmical behaviour pattern	trigger stimulus	importance to animal
squirrel	hibernation	decreasing daylength and temperature	conserves energy when food is in short supply

4. Investigating Cells

Investigating Living Cells

Cells are the basic units of all living things (organisms).

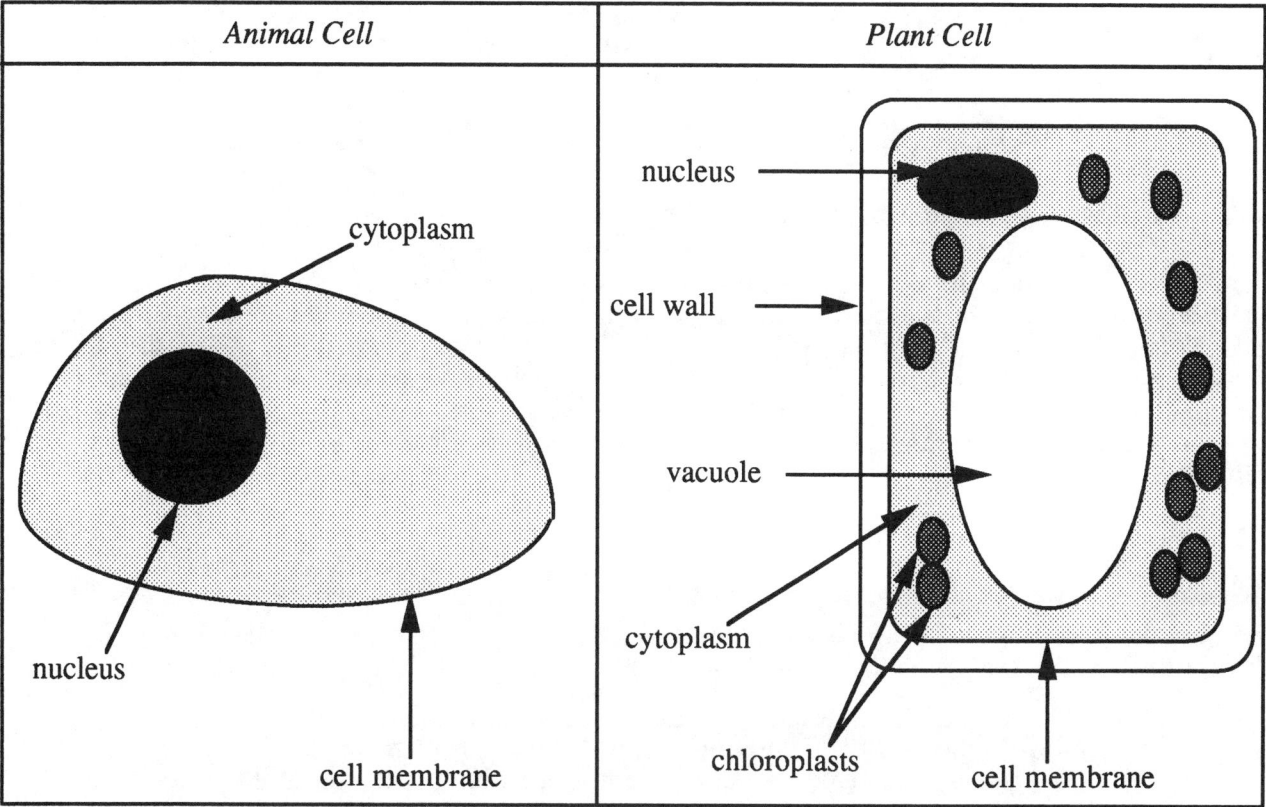

Animal Cell	*Plant Cell*

cytoplasm

nucleus

cell membrane

nucleus

cell wall

vacuole

cytoplasm

chloroplasts

cell membrane

Stains are used in the preparation of microscope slides to make cell structures (such as the nucleus, cytoplasm and cell membrane) more clearly visible.

Investigating Diffusion

Diffusion is the movement of molecules from an area of high concentration to an area of low concentration until they are evenly spread.

1. Diffusion and living cells

Some substances can get into and out of a cell by diffusion through the cell membrane.
Examples of substances that diffuse into or out of a cell are shown below.

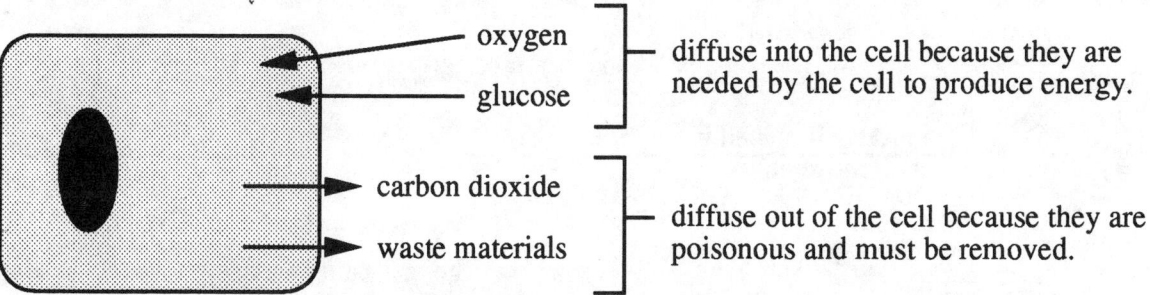

oxygen
glucose

— diffuse into the cell because they are needed by the cell to produce energy.

carbon dioxide
waste materials

— diffuse out of the cell because they are poisonous and must be removed.

2. Diffusion through cell membranes

The cell membrane does not allow all molecules to pass through it. Some molecules are too large to pass through (e.g. sucrose).

Potatoes are made up of many living cells. Each cell is surrounded by a membrane. If pieces of potato are placed in water or strong sucrose solution, they either swell up or shrink. This is because they either gain or lose water.

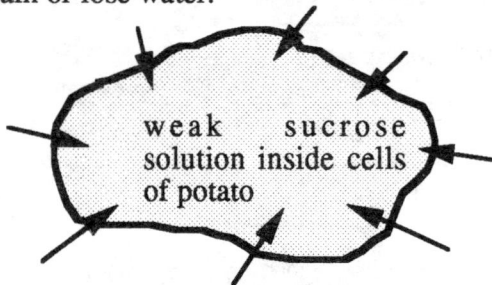

weak sucrose solution inside cells of potato

arrows denote direction of movement of water

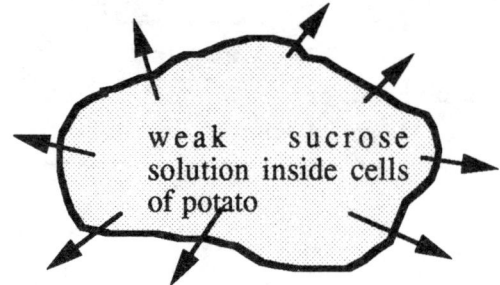

weak sucrose solution inside cells of potato

pure water outside

strong sucrose solution outside

The sucrose molecules are too large to pass easily through the membrane of the potato cells. Water molecules can and they diffuse from the high water concentration outside into the weak sucrose solution (low water concentration) inside the cells. This causes the piece of potato to swell .

The sucrose molecules are too large to pass easily through the membrane of the potato cells. Water molecules can and they diffuse from the weak sucrose solution (high water concentration) to the strong sucrose solution (low water concentration). This causes the potato to shrink.

3. Osmosis

The potatoes shrink or swell up because the cells either lose water or gain water. This movement (diffusion) of water through the cell membrane is a special case of diffusion called **osmosis**.

> Osmosis is the **movement of water** through a cell membrane **from** an area where it is in a **high** concentration **to** an area where it is in a **low** concentration.

4. Osmosis and animal cells

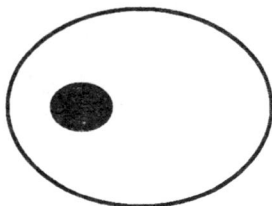

animal cell placed in strong salt or sucrose solution

The cell loses water and becomes shrivelled up.

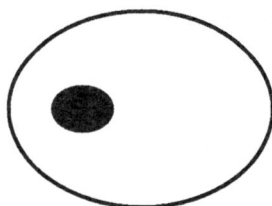

animal cell placed in distilled water

The cell gains water and eventually bursts.

5. Osmosis and plant cells

The vacuole in plant cells contains salts and sucrose dissolved in water to form a weak solution. During osmosis, water can either enter or leave the vacuole depending on the solution surrounding the vacuole.

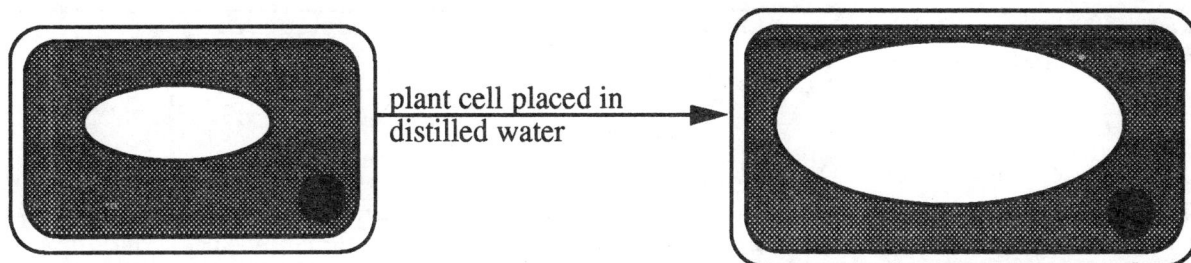

plant cell placed in distilled water

The cell vacuole gains water and the cell becomes swollen (**turgid**).

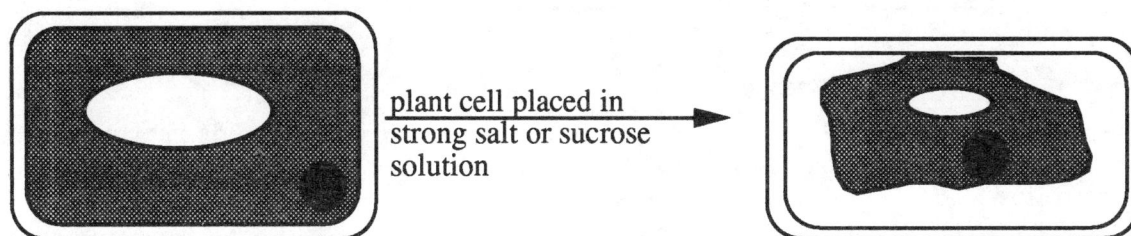

plant cell placed in strong salt or sucrose solution

The cell vacuole loses water and the cytoplasm is pulled away from the cell wall as the vacuole loses water. The cell becomes **plasmolysed**.

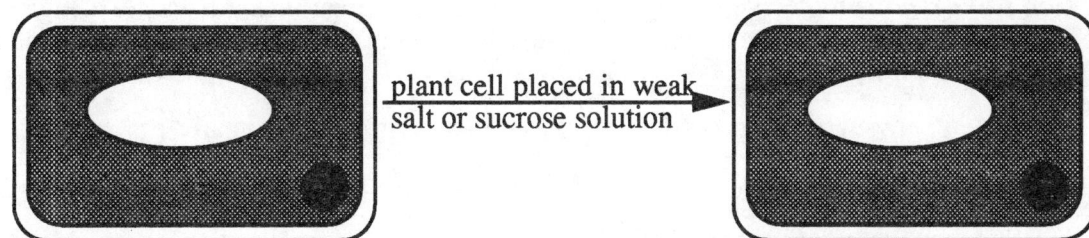

plant cell placed in weak salt or sucrose solution

The cell vacuole stays the same as there is no gain or loss of water.

The cell membrane is described as being **selectively permeable** because it only allows smaller molecules (e.g. water) to pass through it and not larger ones (e.g. sucrose and salt). Molecules which pass through the cell membrane do so because there is a high concentration on one side and a low concentration on the other. This is described as a **concentration gradient**.

Investigating Cell Division

Cell division is an important process which **increases** the number of **cells** in an organism. The way in which cells divide to produce new cells is called **mitosis.**

Mitosis is important because:

   (a) it produces new cells for growth and repair;

   (b) it is the way in which single-celled organisms reproduce.

When a cell is ready to divide, long threads called **chromosomes** appear in the nucleus. These threads contain all the information necessary for the control of the cell and all the instructions necessary to build a whole new organism. When a cell divides, a new set of chromosomes must be made so that the instructions can be passed on to the daughter cells.

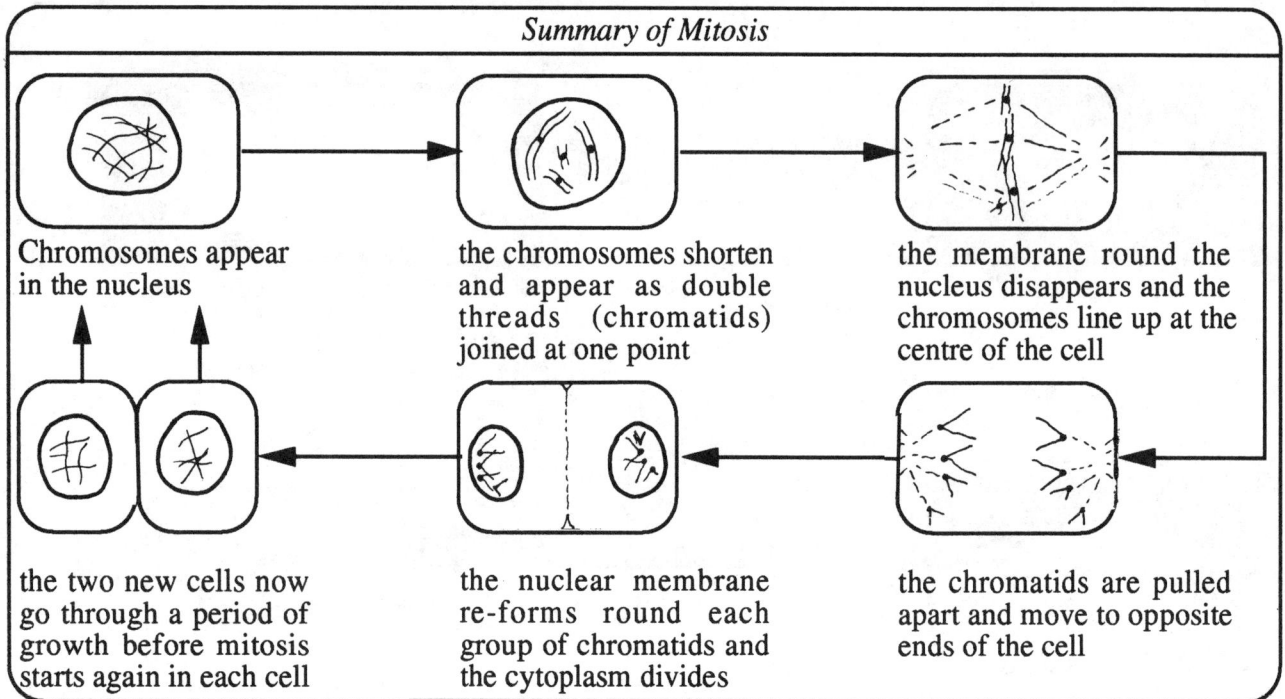

Summary of Mitosis

Chromosomes appear in the nucleus

the chromosomes shorten and appear as double threads (chromatids) joined at one point

the membrane round the nucleus disappears and the chromosomes line up at the centre of the cell

the two new cells now go through a period of growth before mitosis starts again in each cell

the nuclear membrane re-forms round each group of chromatids and the cytoplasm divides

the chromatids are pulled apart and move to opposite ends of the cell

Investigating Enzymes

1. Cell reactions

A chemical reaction is where one molecule, or a group of molecules, change in some way. Chemical reactions occur in cells all the time. An example of one is the changing of hydrogen peroxide into water and oxygen. We would write it this way:

hydrogen peroxide ⟶ water + oxygen

There are two types of reaction:-

(a) **breakdown reactions**: where one molecule breaks down into smaller molecules.

starch ⟶ maltose

(b) **synthesis reactions**: where molecules join together to make a larger molecule.

glucose–1–phosphate ⟶ starch

2. What are enzymes?

Catalysts are chemicals which speed up reactions. Enzymes are catalysts which speed up the reactions that take place in cells. All cell reactions are speeded up, or helped, by enzymes.

The molecule that an enzyme works on is called the **substrate**.

The molecule that is produced is called the **product**.

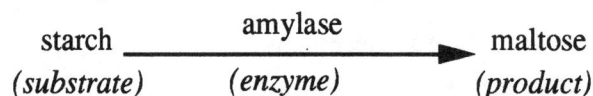

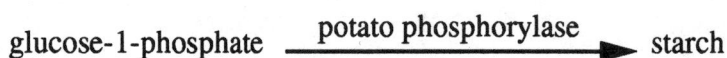

starch $\xrightarrow{\text{amylase}}$ maltose
(substrate) *(enzyme)* *(product)*

glucose-1-phosphate $\xrightarrow{\text{potato phosphorylase}}$ starch

28

3. Some more information about enzymes

(a) Enzymes are made from protein.

(b) They can be used over and over again. They are never used up in reactions.

(c) They are specific. This means that each enzyme can only react with one substrate molecule. For example, the enzyme catalase will only affect the breakdown of hydrogen peroxide into water and oxygen. It does not have an effect on any other reaction.

(d) Enzymes are affected by temperature:

i) They work slower at cold temperatures.

ii) They work faster at warm temperatures.

iii) The temperature they work **best** at is called the **optimum** temperature. The optimum temperature for most mammal enzymes is 37°C. Plant enzymes have an optimum temperature around 20°C.

iv) At high temperatures (over 50°C) enzymes are denatured. This means that they are altered in shape and cannot work.

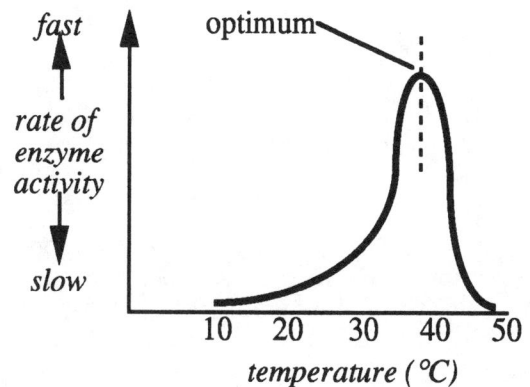

(e) Enzymes are affected by pH. The pH an enzyme works best at is called is optimum pH.

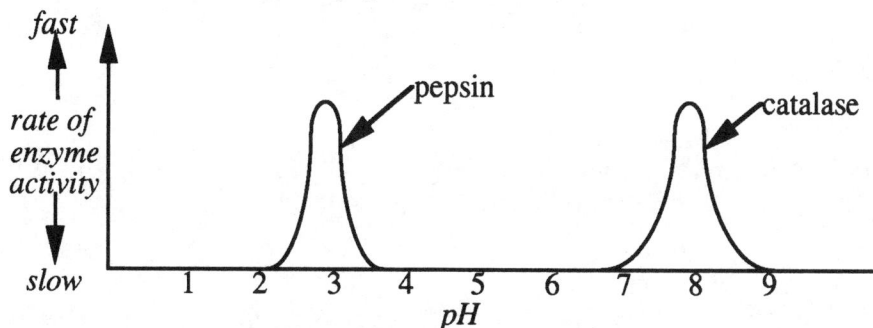

Pepsin works best between pH 2 and pH 4. Its optimum is pH 3.

Catalase works best between pH 7 and pH 9. Its optimum is pH 8.

4. Enzymes and cell chemistry

Almost all the reactions which happen inside an organism are controlled by enzymes. Without enzymes these reactions would go too slowly for life to exist. Enzymes are essential for life. Most processes in an organism consist of many reactions, each of which is controlled by an enzyme. Some of these processes are listed below:

(a) **photosynthesis**;

(b) **respiration**;

(c) **germination**;

(d) **growth**;

(e) **digestion**.

Investigating Aerobic Respiration

Living things need energy to grow and reproduce. They obtain this energy from food. The energy in food is chemical energy. When the food is broken down, it is converted to another form of energy.

chemical energy in food ⟶ **movement energy when you move**

chemical energy in food ⟶ **heat energy to keep you warm**

1. Energy content of food

All foods contain energy, but some contain more than others. Fats and oils contain twice as much energy as proteins and carbohydrates.

> *fats and oils - 38 kJ*
> *carbohydrates - 17kJ*
> *proteins - 22kJ*

Although carbohydrates contain less energy, it is easier to release the energy from them than from fats and proteins. Therefore the body's main energy supply comes from carbohydrate in the form of glucose. The process which releases energy from food is **respiration**.

2. Aerobic respiration

When oxygen is used in respiration, it is described as **aerobic respiration**. What happens in cells is shown in the reaction below:

glucose + oxygen ⟶ **carbon dioxide + water + energy**

The carbon dioxide produced is breathed out.

3. Uses of energy

The energy produced by respiration is often in the form of heat energy, which helps animals keep warm. Energy is also needed for movement and for all the reactions that take place in cells.

4. Measuring respiration

During aerobic respiration, oxygen gas is used up and carbon dioxide gas is produced.

A simple piece of apparatus can be used to show these gas changes during respiration. This piece of apparatus is called a **respirometer**.

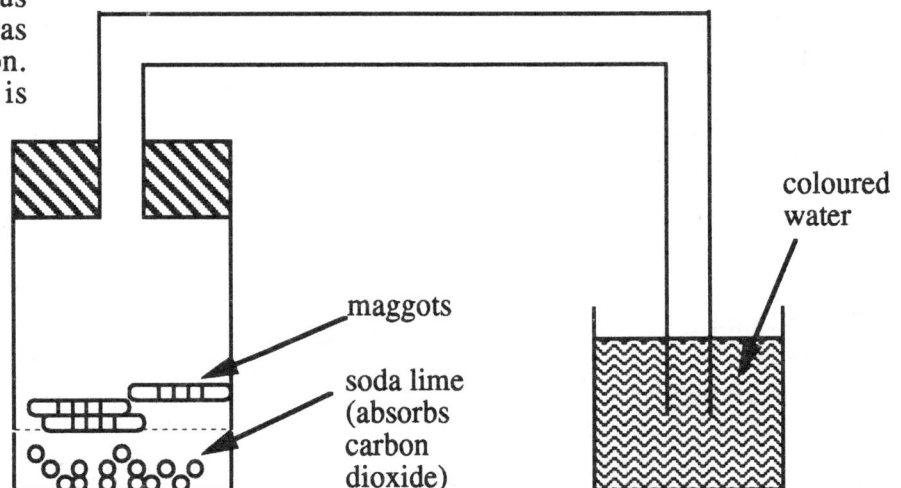

maggots

coloured water

soda lime (absorbs carbon dioxide)

As the oxygen is used up by the maggots, the coloured water moves towards them up the glass tube. The carbon dioxide they breathe out is absorbed by the soda lime and so does not push the water back. We can place the maggots in different conditions (e.g. hot or cold) and compare the rate of movement of the coloured water. This is a measure of the rate of respiration.

30

5. The Body in Action

Movement

Animals must be able to move in order to find food and must have limbs that allow them to move easily.

For physical activity to take place the body requires:

(a) support ;

(b) a means of movement;

(c) energy;

(d) co-ordination.

1. The skeleton

The skeleton has a number of functions:

(a) it keeps the shape of the animal;

(b) it supports their weight;

(c) it protects vital organs such as the brain, heart, lungs and spinal cord;

(d) it provides a framework for the attachment of muscles.

2. The structure of bone

Bones are alive. They are made of living cells. These cells are made of flexible fibres and are surrounded by hard minerals.

The living cells give bones flexibility.

The minerals give bones strength and hardness.

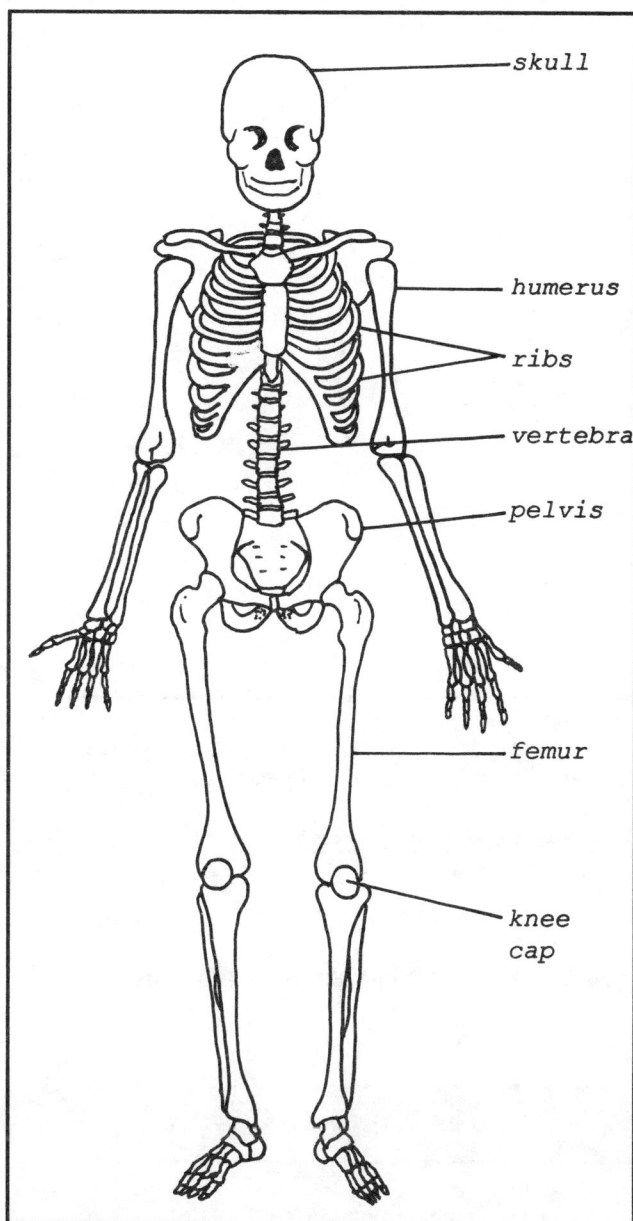

skull
humerus
ribs
vertebra
pelvis
femur
knee cap

3. Joints

A joint is a place where two or more bones meet (e.g. elbow or shoulder).

Different joints in your body allow you to carry out different types of movement.

type of joint	type of movement possible	examples
ball and socket	in all directions	shoulder hip
hinge joint	in one direction (like a hinge)	knee elbow

31

hinge joint	ligament	ball and socket joint

ligament — holds bones together at a joint

synovial membrane — produces synovial fluid

synovial fluid — reduces friction in a joint

cartilage — acts as a shock absorber

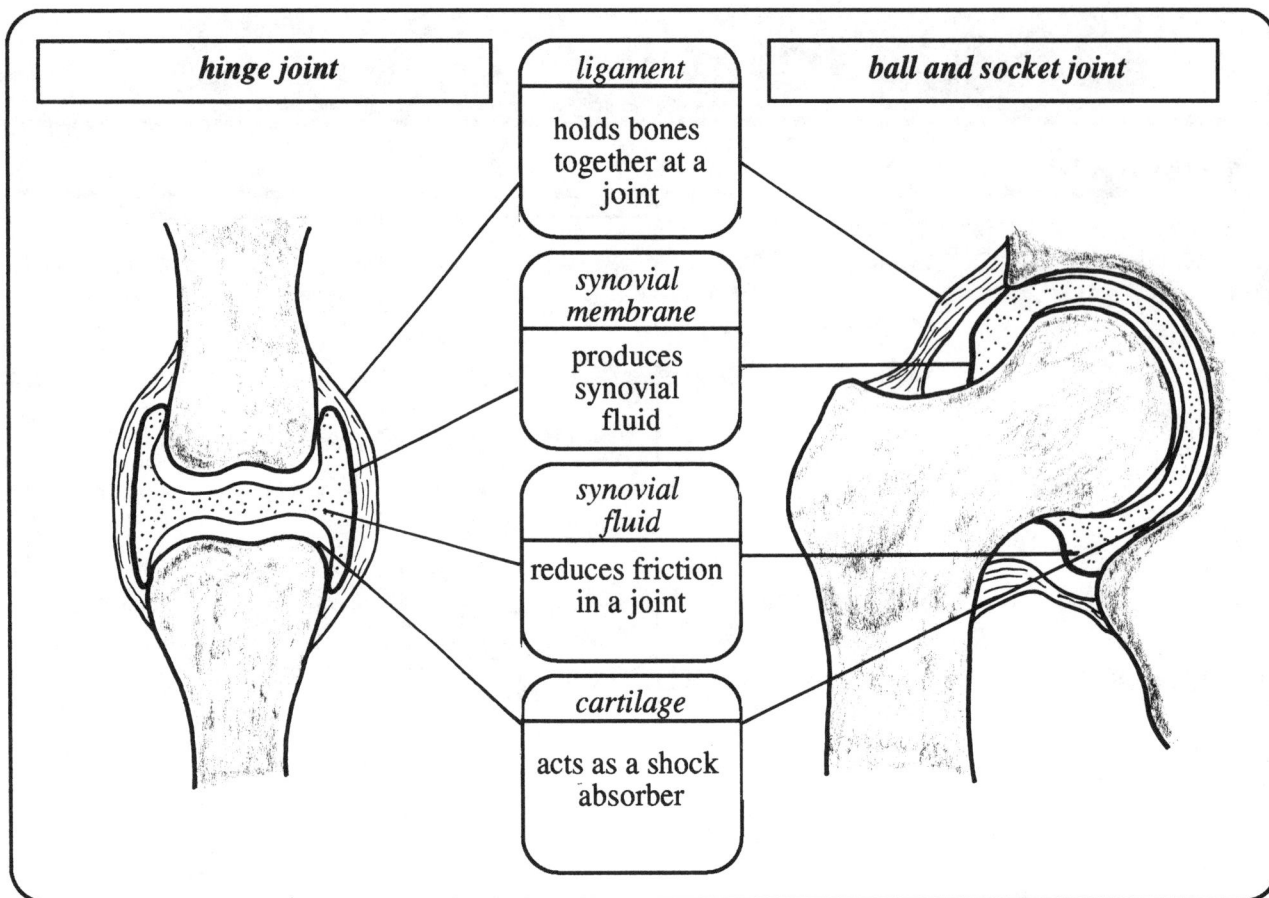

A joint is an efficient structure because friction is reduced by the smooth cartilage and the oily, slippery synovial fluid. The strong fibres of the ligaments allow the joint to withstand shock.

4. Muscles and movement

To allow you to move the entire skeleton is covered in muscle. A muscle works by pulling on a bone. To do this the muscle has to contract (shorten).

Muscles are attached to bones by **tendons.**

Tendons are very strong and do not stretch so that the muscle can pull on the bone.

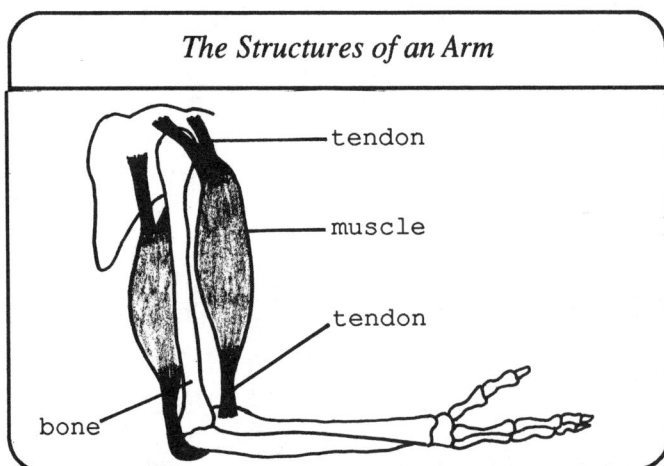

The Structures of an Arm

tendon

muscle

tendon

bone

The muscles at a joint always work in pairs. One muscle makes the joint bend while the other straightens it.

To flex the arm upwards at the elbow, the muscle at the front of the arm contracts. To straighten the arm, the muscle at the back of the upper arm contracts.

Muscles work in pairs - when one of the pair is contracted, the other is relaxed.

5. Sports injuries

If you get involved in a strenuous activity like sport, it is possible to injure your joints, muscles and tendons. Some parts of the body are more likely to be injured than others. The most common injury is to the knee and the least common is to the head and neck. Sports injuries occur because of the sudden changes of movement and the knocks that can happen.

The Need for Energy

Your body needs energy to take part in sport or any other activity that involves movement.

Different foods contain different amounts of energy. To release the energy in food, it must be combined with oxygen in our bodies. During this process, carbon dioxide is produced as a waste product.

If a person's energy input (i.e. food intake) is higher than their energy output then their body stores this extra energy in the form of fat. If a person's energy output is higher that their energy input, then they will lose weight.

1. The structure of lungs

The oxygen you need to release energy from food is obtained by breathing in.
The carbon dioxide produced as a waste product is removed by breathing out.

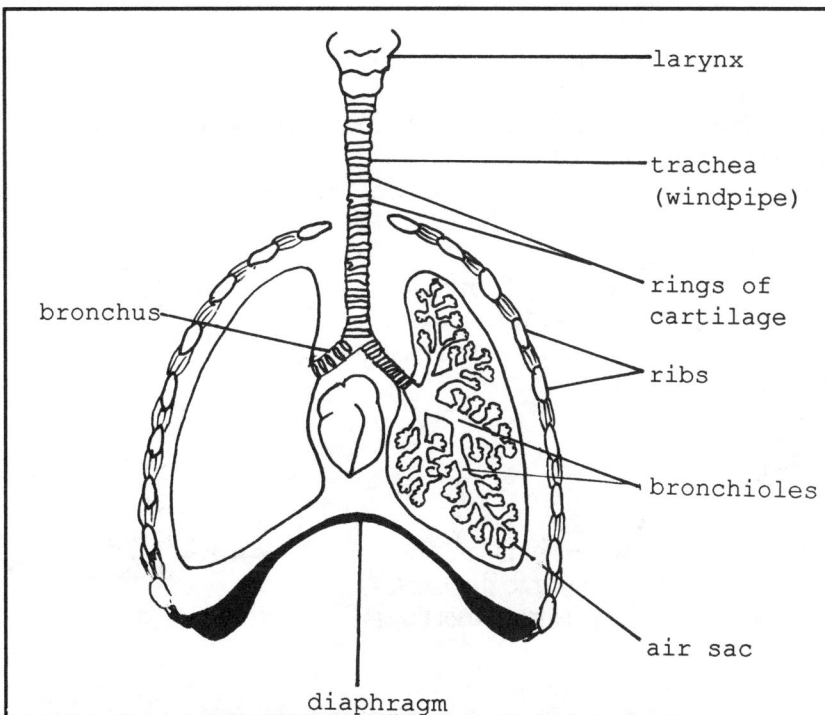

Air comes in at the mouth and passes down the trachea. On the way, it passes through the larynx (voice box). The trachea is held open by rings of cartilage. The air then passes down a bronchus, which divides into many tiny tubes called bronchioles. The bronchioles end in air sacs.

2. Gas exchange in the air sacs

The air sacs are lined with moisture. Oxygen, in the breathed-in air, dissolves in this moisture and diffuses into the blood. Carbon dioxide diffuses in the opposite direction from the capillary into the air sac.

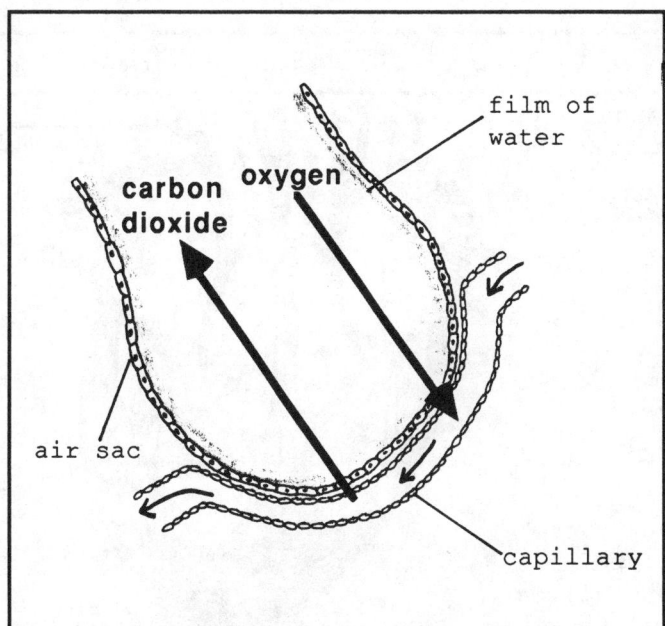

Whenever gases are exchanged, three conditions are necessary if the gases are to be exchanged efficiently. These are:

(a) **large surface** - there are many air sacs

(b) **thin surface** - the air sac and capillary are only one cell thick

(c) **moist surface** - film of water inside the air sac

33

3. Cleaning breathed-in air

The air you breathe in often contains dust and germs which must not be allowed to enter the lungs. The air entering the lungs is cleaned by special cells lining the air tubes. These cells have small hairs, called cilia, which beat in waves. A slippery liquid, called mucus, is also made by these cells. This mucus traps the dirt and germs. The cilia beat and move the mucus towards the mouth. In this way, dirt and germs are carried up to the mouth and then swallowed.

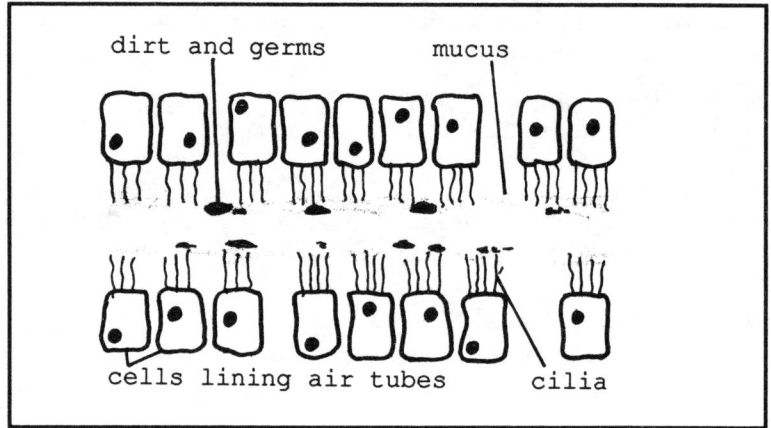

4. Breathing movements

When we breathe, our chest moves in and out like a pair of bellows. Your ribs move up and out, and down and in. At the same time, your diaphragm also moves.

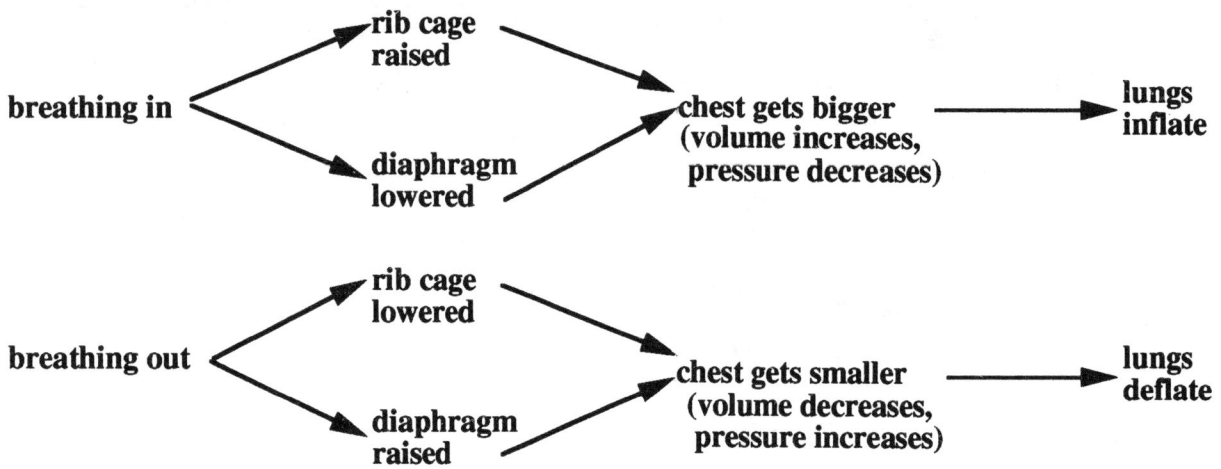

breathing in → **rib cage raised** / **diaphragm lowered** → **chest gets bigger (volume increases, pressure decreases)** → **lungs inflate**

breathing out → **rib cage lowered** / **diaphragm raised** → **chest gets smaller (volume decreases, pressure increases)** → **lungs deflate**

5. Heart structure

Once oxygen enters the body, it has to be carried to all the cells of the body. It is carried by blood in the blood vessels. The heart pumps the blood around the body.

The power required by the heart to pump blood around the body is produced by muscles in its wall.

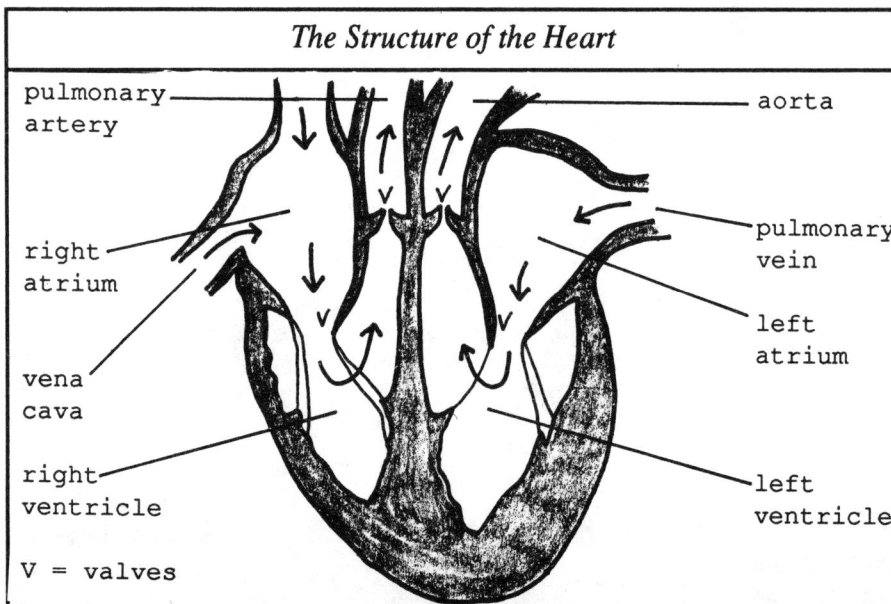

The Structure of the Heart

pulmonary artery — aorta — right atrium — pulmonary vein — vena cava — left atrium — right ventricle — left ventricle — V = valves

The function of the heart valves is to keep blood flowing in one direction and stop backflow.

The wall of the left ventricle is thicker than the right ventricle because it has to pump blood all around the body. The right ventricle only pumps blood to the lungs.

The heart gets its own blood supply from the coronary arteries which run over its surface.

34

The flow chart below shows the path taken by blood on its way through the heart to the lungs, back to the heart and out to the body.

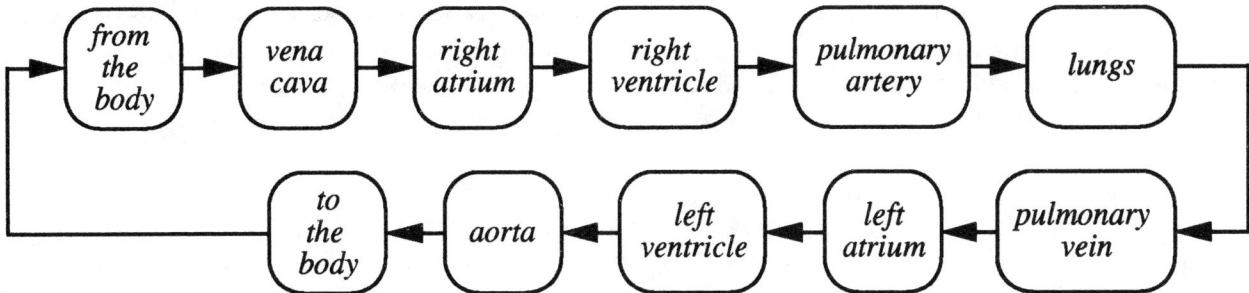

```
from the body → vena cava → right atrium → right ventricle → pulmonary artery → lungs
to the body ← aorta ← left ventricle ← left atrium ← pulmonary vein
```

6. Blood vessels

Blood is carried all around the body in blood vessels. Blood leaves the heart and is carried in arteries. The arteries branch into tiny tubes called capillaries. The capillaries then join up to form veins which carry blood back to the heart.

Each time your heart beats blood is pushed along the arteries. This can be felt when you take your pulse.

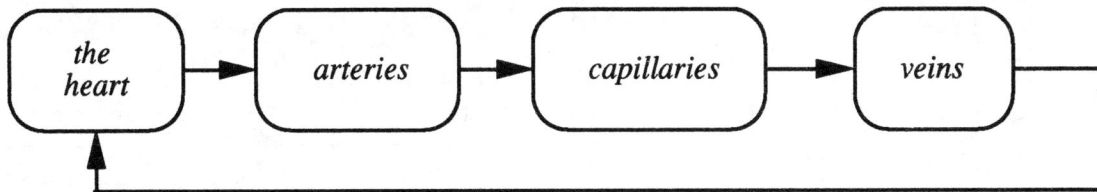

```
the heart → arteries → capillaries → veins
```

As blood flows through the capillaries, oxygen diffuses from the capillaries into the body cells. In exchange, carbon dioxide diffuses from the body cells into the capillaries. As with gas exchange in the air sacs, the same three conditions are required for gas exchange in the capillaries. These are:

(a) large surface - many capillaries;

(b) thin surface - capillaries are only one cell thick;

(c) moist surface - body cells are all bathed in a fluid;

7. Blood

Blood is made up of cells floating in a liquid called plasma.

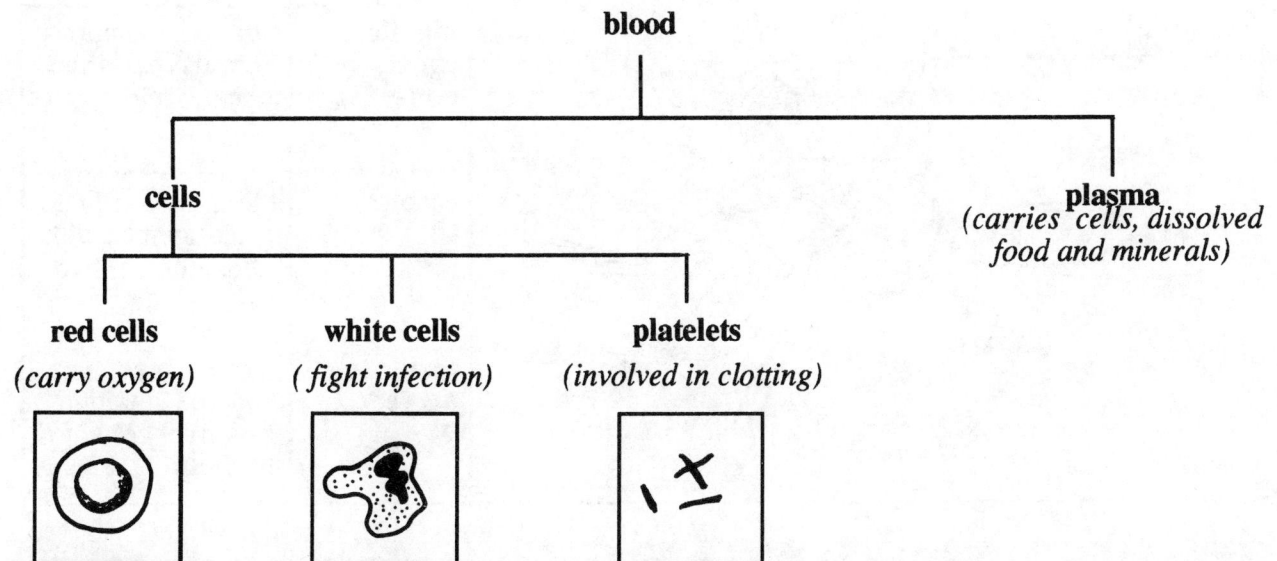

```
                    blood
          ┌───────────┴───────────┐
        cells                   plasma
                          (carries cells, dissolved
                              food and minerals)
     ┌──────┼──────┐
red cells  white cells  platelets
(carry     (fight      (involved in clotting)
oxygen)    infection)
```

Red cells carry oxygen round the body. They contain the chemical **haemoglobin.** Haemoglobin combine with oxygen to form **oxy-haemoglobin.** In the capillaries, the oxygen is released from the haemoglobin and diffuses into the body cells.

Co-ordination

Our nervous system controls every action we make. The sense organs respond to information from our surroundings (e.g. sound and light) and send messages to our brain and spinal cord. The brain and spinal cord sort out this information and send instructions to the body, which then responds.

1. The eye

The eye is the sense organ you use to detect light. Your eyes also allow you to judge distances. This can be done more accurately using two eyes rather than one. Each eye sees a slightly different view. The brain puts these two views together to form a three-dimensional view which helps in the judgement of distances. This is called **binocular vision**.

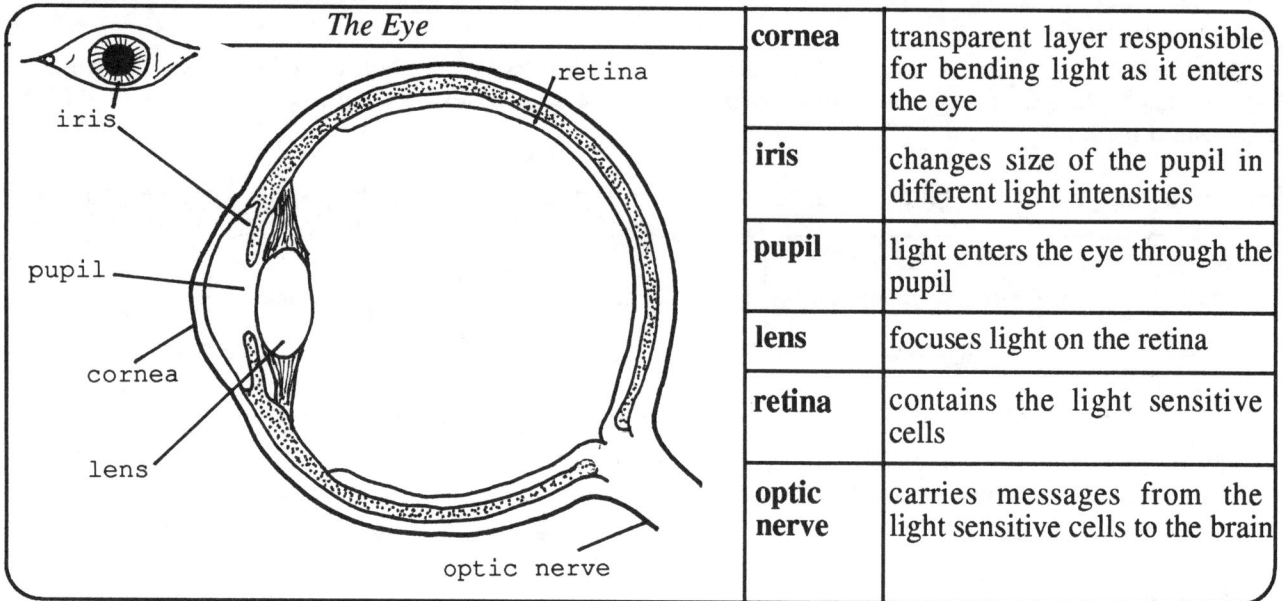

The Eye

cornea	transparent layer responsible for bending light as it enters the eye
iris	changes size of the pupil in different light intensities
pupil	light enters the eye through the pupil
lens	focuses light on the retina
retina	contains the light sensitive cells
optic nerve	carries messages from the light sensitive cells to the brain

2. The ear

The ear is the sense-organ used to detect sound. Our judgement of sound is made more accurate by having two ears.

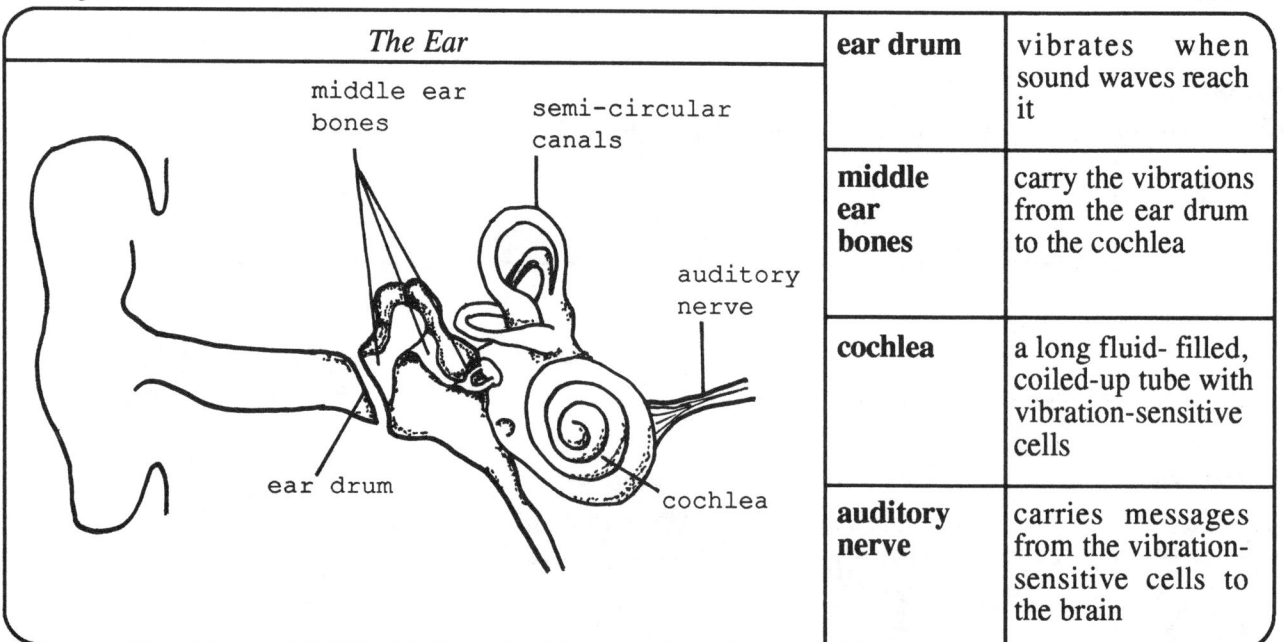

The Ear

ear drum	vibrates when sound waves reach it
middle ear bones	carry the vibrations from the ear drum to the cochlea
cochlea	a long fluid-filled, coiled-up tube with vibration-sensitive cells
auditory nerve	carries messages from the vibration-sensitive cells to the brain

3. Balance

The semi-circular canals help you to keep your balance. They are three tubes each at right angles to each other. When you move your head, cells in the walls of the canals pick up the movement of fluid in the canals and send messages to your brain.

4. The nervous system

The nervous system controls the body. It consists of the brain, spinal cord and nerves.

Nerves are made up of many nerve cells. Nerve cells are stretched out into long, thin fibres that can be over one metre long. Nerve impulses travel along nerve cell fibres in one direction. There are three types of nerve cells which are involved in the flow of information. These are shown in the diagram below.

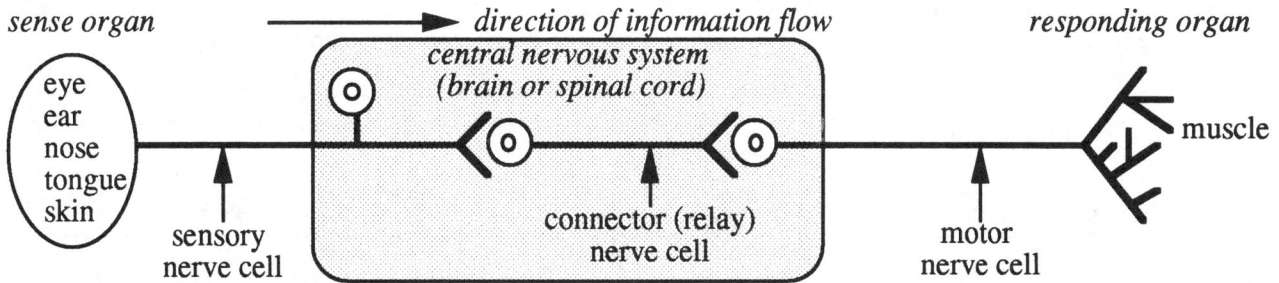

A stimulus (e.g. heat) is detected by the sense organ and a nerve impulse is sent along the sensory nerve cell to the central nervous system. The central nervous system works out the best response and sends an impulse along the motor nerve cell to the muscle. The muscle responds by contracting.

5. A reflex action

A reflex action is a rapid, automatic response to a stimulus which is usually dangerous. It protects the body by allowing it to react quickly. A reflex action involves a flow of information into and out of the spinal cord only involving the brain after the action has taken place.
This is called a **reflex arc** and is shown in the diagram below.

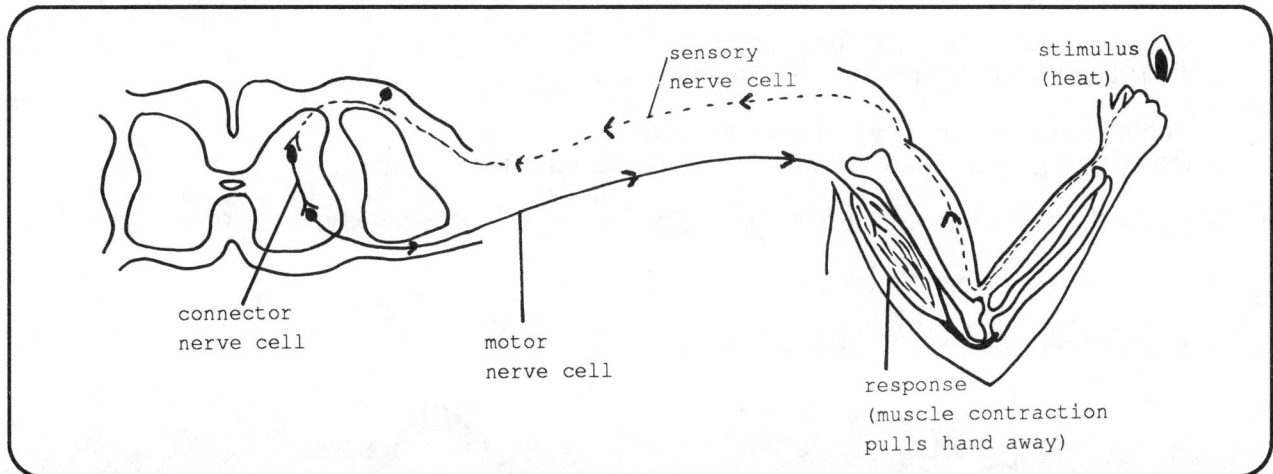

6. The brain

The brain is at the top of the spinal cord and is protected by the skull.

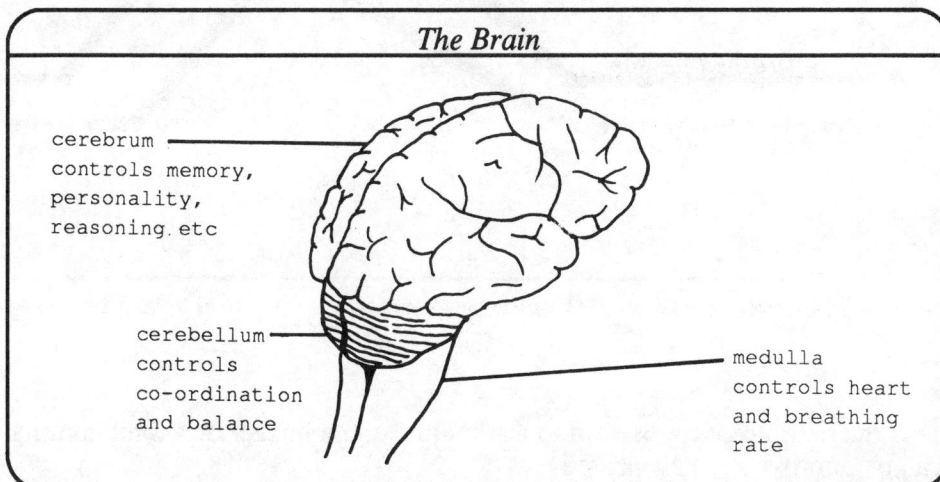

Changing Levels of Performance

1. Exercise and fatigue

When you run fast, your muscles use up lots of glucose in producing energy. Sometimes not enough oxygen gets to your muscles, so respiration without oxygen (**anaerobic respiration**) takes place. Instead of being broken down to carbon dioxide and water, glucose is broken down into a chemical called **lactic acid**. Lactic acid builds up in your muscles and causes soreness and fatigue.

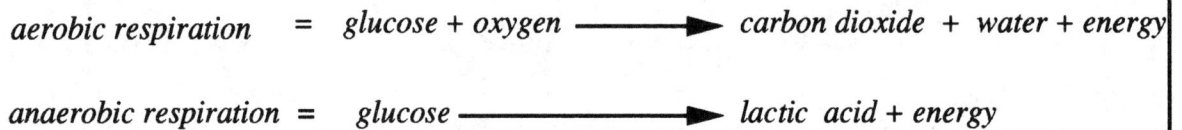

$$aerobic \; respiration \quad = \quad glucose + oxygen \longrightarrow carbon \; dioxide \; + \; water + energy$$

$$anaerobic \; respiration \; = \quad glucose \longrightarrow lactic \; acid + energy$$

At the end of the exercise, you get rid of the lactic acid by breathing rapidly to take in more oxygen. The lactic acid then breaks down to carbon dioxide and water. The amount of oxygen you need to breathe in to break down the lactic acid is called the **oxygen debt**.

2. The effects of training

When you exercise, your pulse and breathing rate increase. This means that your heart is beating faster to carry more food and oxygen to the contracting muscles. Your breathing rate also increases. The recovery time is the time taken for the pulse and breathing rate to return to normal.

Training has the following effects on the body:

(a)   it increases heart volume and the amount of blood sent out
       during each beat, causing a lower resting pulse rate;

(b)   it increases lung volume and so increases the amount of oxygen
       taken in during each breath, causing a lower breathing rate;

(c)   it produces a faster recovery time as lactic acid is removed more quickly;

(d)   it improves circulation to muscles.

This training effect is shown in the diagram below.

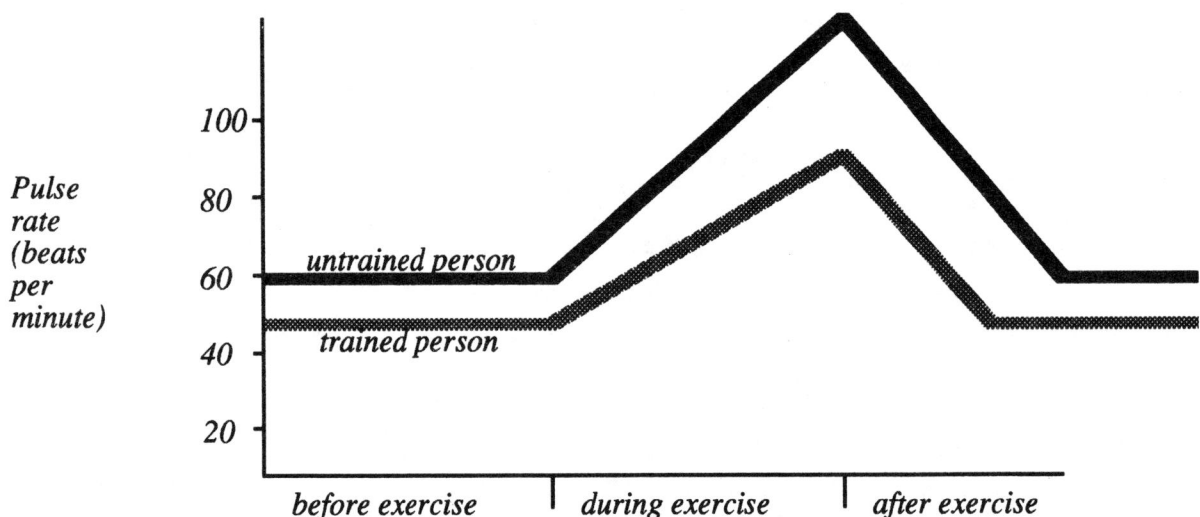

3. Reaction time

The reaction time is the time taken to respond to a stimulus (e.g. a buzzer or a light coming on). Reaction times can be improved after repeated practice.

6. Inheritance

Variation

No two people are exactly alike. Differences exist between all people. In other words, variation occurs between individuals.

There are two types of variation:

(1)   continuous variation;   (2)   discontinuous variation.

1. Continuous variation

This type of variation contains no distinct groups of people and any differences between people can be measured. Within a large group, any characteristic will vary from one extreme to another, e.g. from very small to very tall.

A large group can be surveyed for a particular characteristic which is an example of continuous variation. The results can then be displayed as a graph. The shape of the graph may be like the two drawn below.

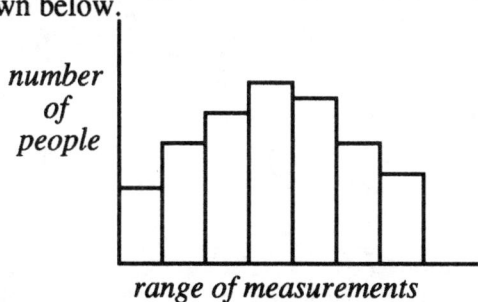   or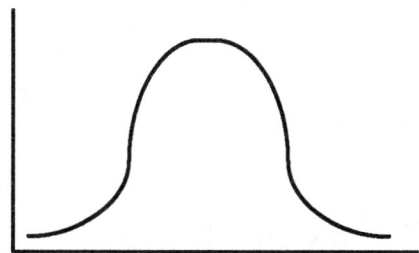

A histogram   **A line graph**

Typical examples of continuous variation are pulse rate (beats per minute), height, weight and handspan.

2. Discontinuous variation

In this type of variation, individuals can be divided into two or more distinct groups.

A survey of a large group may produce the following types of graphs:

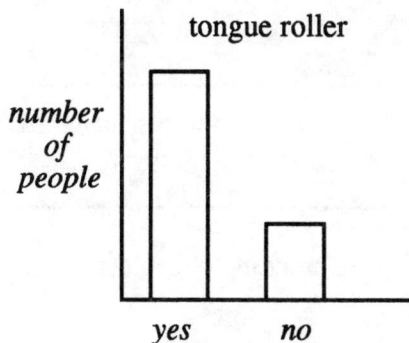   or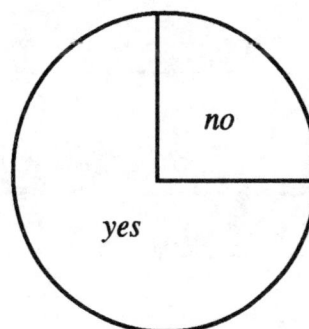

A bar chart   **A pie chart**

3. What is a species?

> A species is a group of living things that are so similar to each other that:
>
> (a)   they are able to interbreed and produce offspring;
>
> (b)   the offspring are fertile (able to produce offspring of their own).

What is Inheritance?

All characteristics (e.g. hair colour, blood group, colour of flowers) are determined by genetic information. This information is carried on the chromosomes found in the nucleus of every cell.

Each parent passes some genetic information to their offspring.

1. Inherited characteristics

Characteristics can exist in different forms, for example:

Organism	Characteristic	Possible form (phenotype)
person	eye colour	blue, brown
	blood group	A, B, O, AB
fruit fly	wing length	long, short
	eye colour	red, white
pea plant	seed shape	round, wrinkled
	seed colour	green, yellow

The possible forms of each characteristic are called the **phenotypes**. The phenotype is the appearance of the organism.

2. Passing on characteristics

If an organism with a particular phenotype is crossed (mated) with another which shows the same phenotype, it can produce offspring which all show the same phenotype.
If only that phenotype, and no other, appears in the next generations, the original organisms are described as **true breeding**.

e.g. A male black mouse is mated with a female black mouse.

If the offspring all have black coats and all subsequent offspring have black coats, then the parents are true breeding.

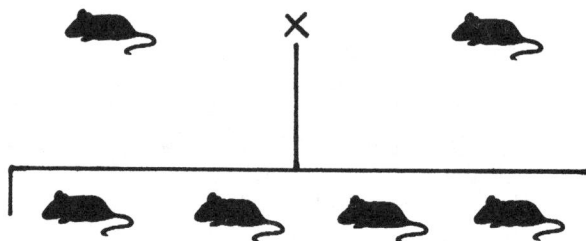

If a true breeding black mouse is crossed with a true breeding chocolate mouse the offspring are all black.

P1 (parents) ⟶ true breeding black x true breeding chocolate

F1 (first generation) →

All the offspring are black because this is the 'stronger' phenotype.
The phenotype 'black coat' is described as **dominant**. The phenotype 'chocolate coat' is described as **recessive**.

If two of the F1 offspring are crossed with each other then the next generation, the F2, will have some black and chocolate coated mice. There will, however, always be more black coated mice. If large numbers of offspring are produced, the ratio of black (dominant) to chocolate (recessive) will be 3 : 1.

3. Chromosome sets and genes

The sex cells (gametes) contain only one set of chromosomes. When fertilisation takes place, the chromosome set of the egg joins with the chromosome set of the sperm. The nucleus of the fertilised egg (zygote) now contains two matching sets of chromosomes. The zygote divides to produce all the other cells of the body. This means that every cell has the same two sets of chromosomes.

When the two sets of chromosomes are examined, they can be arranged in pairs - one of the pair will have come from the mother and the other from the father.

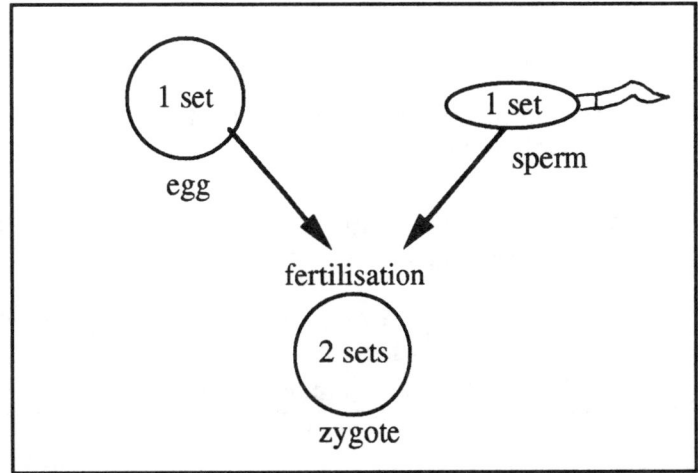

Each chromosome carries information on many tiny units called **genes.** It is these genes that determine the characteristics of an organism.

All characteristics are determined by a pair of genes. The genes for each characteristic exist in two forms (**alleles**). One form is usually dominant and the other is recessive. One example in people is tongue rolling. There are two tongue rolling genes. One gene allows you to roll your tongue. The other gene does not. Depending on which combination of these genes your cells contain, you either can or cannot roll your tongue. The tongue rolling gene is dominant to the non-roller gene.

characteristic of person	tongue roller	tongue roller	non tongue roller
genes contained in body cells	tongue rolling gene tongue rolling gene	tongue rolling gene non rolling gene	non rolling gene non rolling gene

The diagram below shows how the coat colour genes are passed on when true breeding mice are crossed.

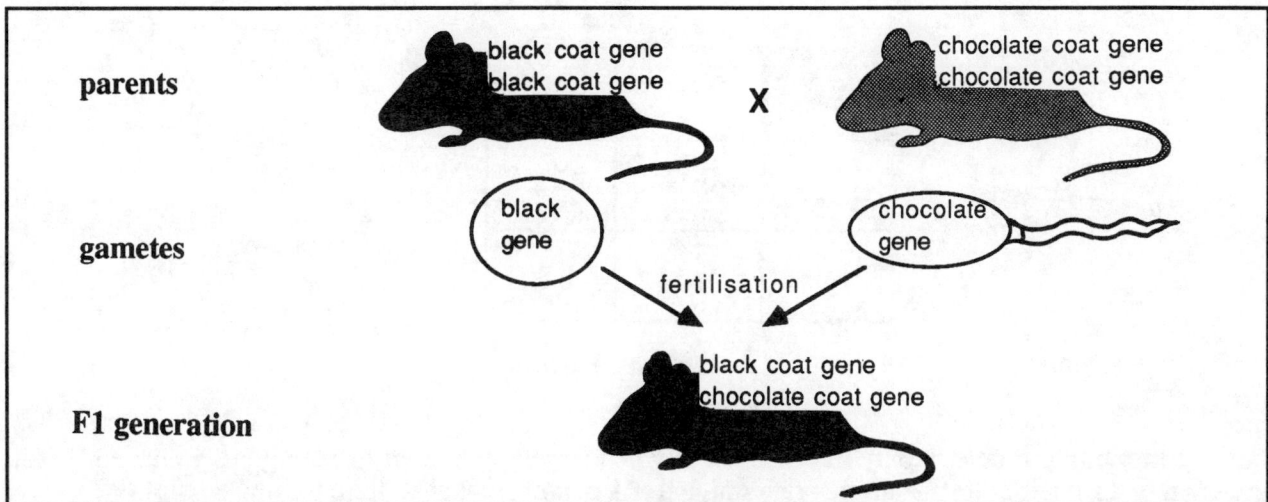

4. The monohybrid cross

The two forms of a particular gene are represented by letters. The dominant allele is always represented by a capital letter and the recessive allele by a small letter.

Tallness in pea plants is dominant to dwarfness. These alleles are represented as follows:

T = tallness   **t = dwarfness**

Each characteristic of an organism is determined by two alleles. The two alleles present in an organism are known as its **genotype**.

A tall pea plant has the genotype TT or Tt.
A dwarf pea plant has the genotype tt.

If the two alleles are the same (TT or tt), the genotype is described as **homozygous.**
If the two alleles are different (Tt), the genotype is described as **heterozygous**.

phenotype	genotype	description of genotype
tall	TT	homozygous dominant
tall	Tt	heterozygous dominant
dwarf	tt	homozygous recessive

The simplest genetic cross involves one characteristic and is called a **monohybrid cross**:

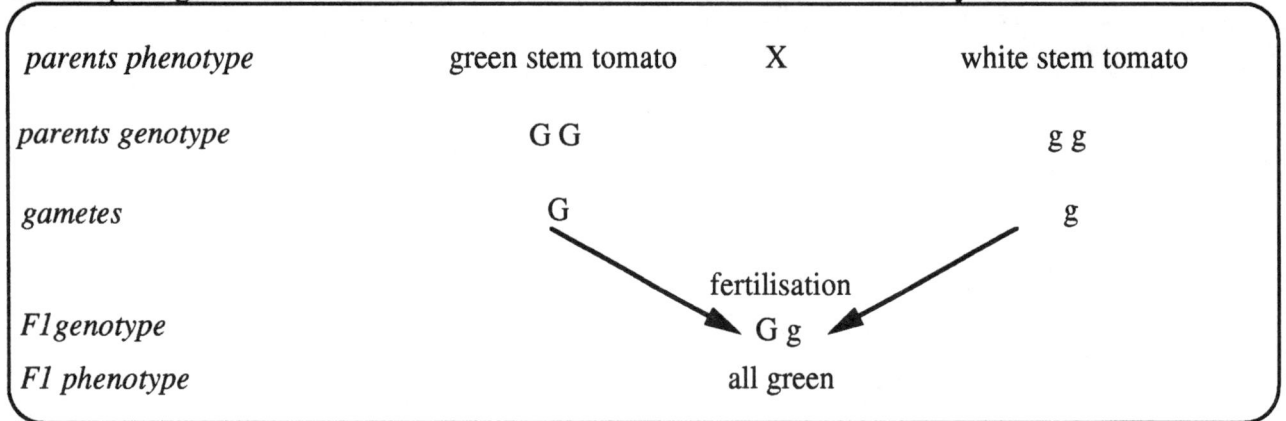

parents phenotype	green stem tomato	X	white stem tomato
parents genotype	G G		g g
gametes	G		g
		fertilisation	
F1 genotype		G g	
F1 phenotype		all green	

The next step involves crossing two individuals from the F1 generation:

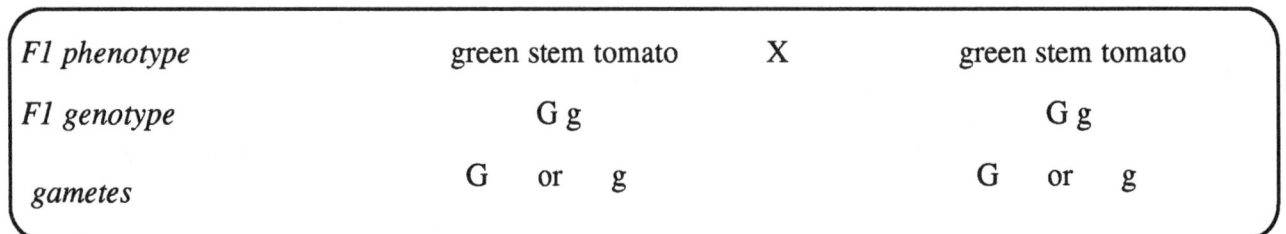

F1 phenotype	green stem tomato	X	green stem tomato
F1 genotype	G g		G g
gametes	G or g		G or g

A punnet square is then used to show the possible ways in which these two sets of gametes could combine during fertilisation:

female gametes

		G	g
male gametes	**G**	**G G** green	**G g** green
	g	**G g** green	**g g** white

F2 genotypes

F2 phenotype ratio   **3 green : 1 white**

The 3 : 1 monohybrid ratio is only likely to occur when large numbers of offspring are produced. Also, the fusion of gametes at fertilisation is random and is a matter of chance (like tossing a coin).

5. Sex determination

A person's sex is determined by a pair of chromosomes, the sex chromosomes. They are called the X and Y chromosomes.

A female has the genotype XX.

A male has the genotype XY.

The diagram opposite shows how sex is inherited.

The ratio of girls to boys is 1 : 1

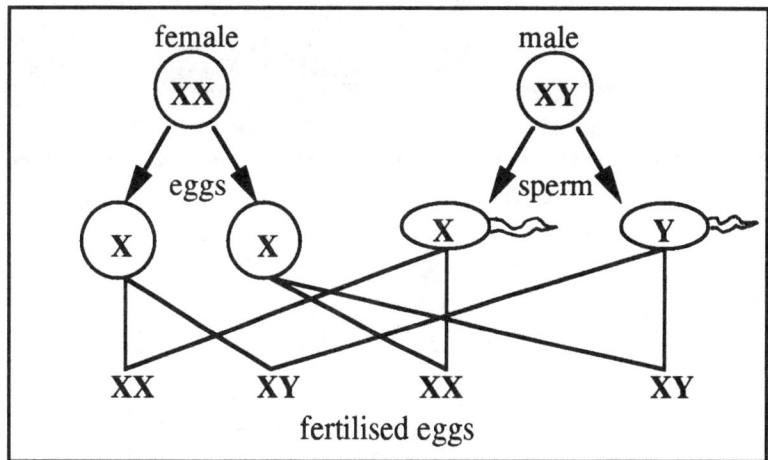

Genetics and Society

1. Selective breeding

For centuries, animal and plant breeders have tried to improve their stock and their crops (e.g. dairy farmers want to have cows which produce large quantities of milk). Improved charcteristics can be obtained by selective breeding. Breeders select and breed those varieties of animals and plants with characteristics that are useful. Selective breeding has resulted in, for example:

      (a)   Aberdeen Angus cattle bred for beef production;

      (b)   sheep bred to produce better wool;

      (c)   poultry bred to grow more quickly;

      (d)   cereals bred to be more resistant to disease.

2. Mutations

Almost 1% of all babies are born with some sort of change to their chromosomes. These changes are called mutations. Down's Syndrome, for example, is caused by a chromosome mutation. Children with Down's Syndrome have an extra chromosome (47 instead of 46).

Mutations occur naturally, but are rare. Radiation, such as X-rays and fall-out from atomic bombs, can increase mutation rate.

Not all mutations are harmful. Some can be useful. Extra chromosomes in spinach and sugar beet, for example, make these plants grow stronger.

3. Amniocentesis

A technique called amniocentesis can be used to detect chromosome changes in an embryo.

A sample of amniotic fluid can be removed using a special syringe. The fluid contains cells from the baby's skin and chemicals from the lungs and urine. The cells can be grown in the lab and then examined to see if there are any defects in the chromosomes. The fluid can be tested to see if it contains certain chemicals which may indicate a chromosome abnormality.

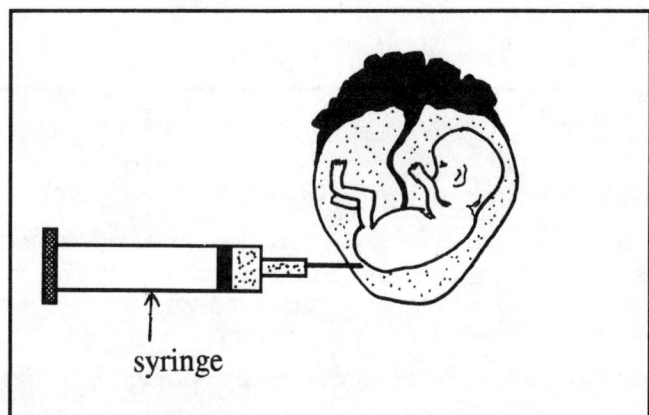

7. Biotechnology

Living Factories

Biotechnology uses living cells to convert raw materials into useful substances. The living cells may come from plants, animals or micro-organisms.

1. Fermentation

Yeast is a living organism. It is a single celled fungus which can feed and grow on sugar. Yeast can respire anaerobically. This means that it breaks down sugars (e.g. glucose) to release energy without using oxygen. As it does this, it also produces carbon dioxide and alcohol.

This process is called fermentation and is summarised in the word equation below.

$$glucose \longrightarrow carbon\ dioxide\ +\ alcohol\ +\ energy$$

Yeast is important in baking because the carbon dioxide produced makes the bread rise. Baking the bread finally kills the yeast and cooks the dough. Alcohol is the useful product of fermentation used in brewing and wine making.

2. Batch processing

Allowing yeast to ferment sugar can be done on a large scale. Batch processing is a technique used by commercial brewers. A large reactor vessel (**a fermenter**) is filled with the necessary raw materials and given the best conditions to promote fermentation.

After the fermenter has been set up, the system is closed and left until fermentation is complete. Then the products can be collected and purified.

Ideally yeast likes conditions where the temperature is between 10° and 18° C, with adequate amounts of glucose and oxygen and a pH of 7. An absence of other micro-organisms (sterile conditions) is essential as these may slow down the process.

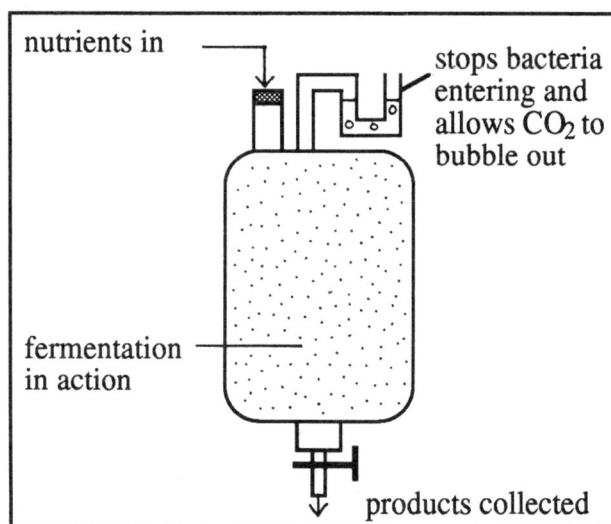

nutrients in

stops bacteria entering and allows CO_2 to bubble out

fermentation in action

products collected

3. The malting of beer

To make beer, brewers use barley as food for yeast. However, barley grains contain starch and not the simple sugar yeast can feed on. The barley must be allowed to germinate in moist, warm conditions in a process called malting. During this time, enzymes present in the barley break down the starch into the sugar maltose which the yeast can feed on.

$$starch \xrightarrow{\text{enzymes in barley grains}} maltose \xrightarrow{\text{yeast}} carbon\ dioxide\ +\ alcohol\ +\ energy$$

4. Other fermentation processes

Fresh milk contains a sugar called lactose. When bacteria feed on this sugar, they break it down in a fermentation process and produce lactic acid. This acid makes the milk go sour. The pH of the milk becomes more and more acidic as more lactose is fermented.

Yoghurt and cheese are produced by adding particular types of bacteria to milk.

Problems and Profit with Waste

Microbes (micro-organisms) are tiny living things that can only be seen using a microscope. They include bacteria, viruses and fungi. Microbes can be useful, but they can also be harmful.

1. Working with microbes

Certain precautions have to be taken when working with microbes to ensure unwanted microbes are not able to grow and cause disease.

Safe Handling of Microbes	
(a) Wash hands and lab bench.	(c) Never open dishes containing microbes.
(b) Always use sterile equipment.	(d) Always dispose of dishes containing microbes by using high temperatures.

Contamination is the presence of unwanted, possibly harmful microbes. Many manufacturing processes (e.g. brewing) have to take special precautions to ensure that all equipment is clean and sterile. After every batch of beer is brewed the equipment is sterilised by using steam heat and chemicals. This is to destroy resistant fungi and bacteria which other methods of sterilisation do not kill.

2. Microbes and decay

After a plant or animal has died, its tissues decay. It is microbes which cause decay. The microbes use the dead material as their food source to obtain energy and building materials to stay alive and grow. These microbes, called **decomposers**, can only use organic (natural) substances. Substances such as plastic do not decay easily.

3. The treatment of sewage

Untreated sewage contains faeces, detergents, food fragments and bacteria which can cause great damage if dumped into a river. Some of these effects are shown below:

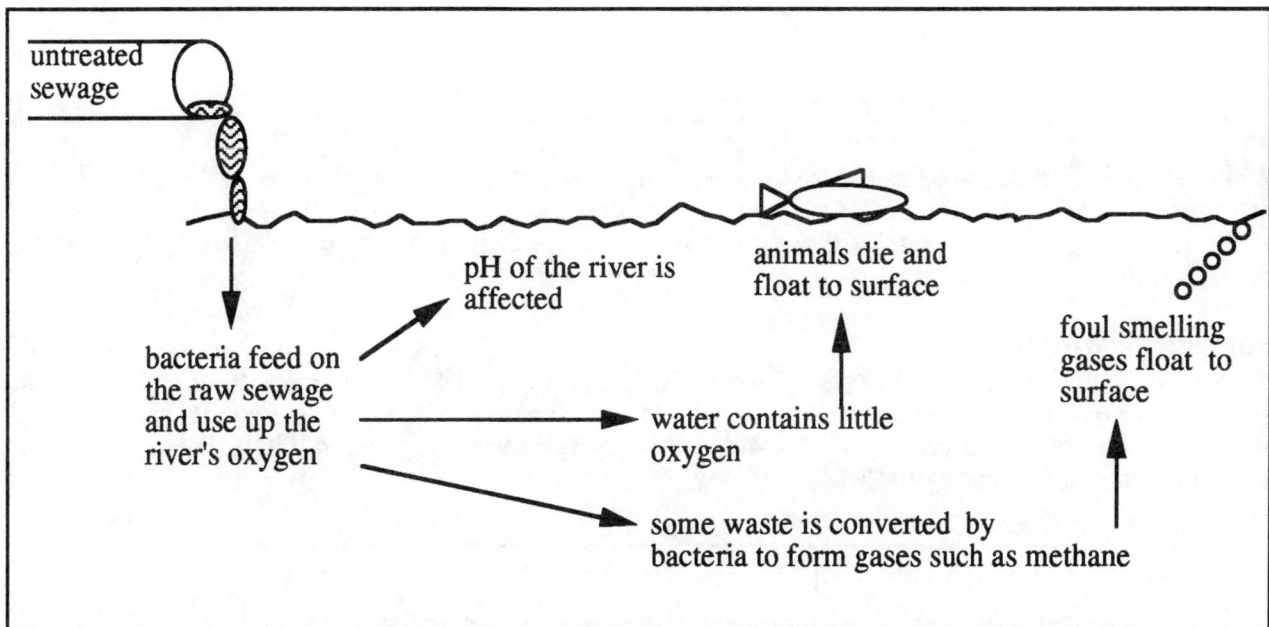

Some of the microbes in sewage cause diseases such as dysentry, typhoid, cholera and food poisoning.

The treatment of sewage involves the conversion of harmful materials to harmless products by the use of microbes.

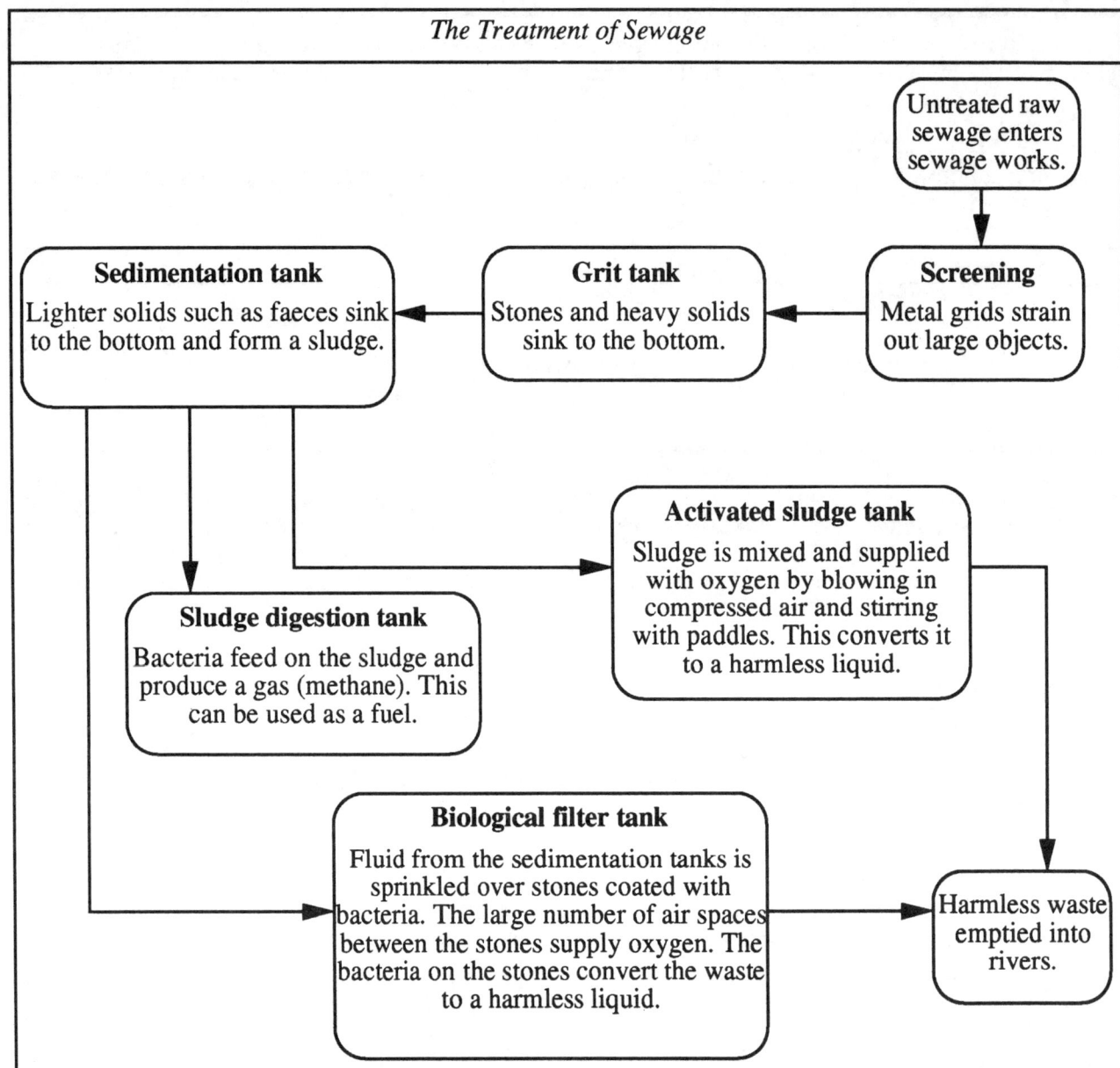

The Treatment of Sewage

Untreated raw sewage enters sewage works.

Screening
Metal grids strain out large objects.

Grit tank
Stones and heavy solids sink to the bottom.

Sedimentation tank
Lighter solids such as faeces sink to the bottom and form a sludge.

Sludge digestion tank
Bacteria feed on the sludge and produce a gas (methane). This can be used as a fuel.

Activated sludge tank
Sludge is mixed and supplied with oxygen by blowing in compressed air and stirring with paddles. This converts it to a harmless liquid.

Biological filter tank
Fluid from the sedimentation tanks is sprinkled over stones coated with bacteria. The large number of air spaces between the stones supply oxygen. The bacteria on the stones convert the waste to a harmless liquid.

Harmless waste emptied into rivers.

Many types of bacteria are used in sewage treatment to ensure the complete breakdown of all the different substances present in the sewage. Complete breakdown is only possible when oxygen is present for aerobic respiration. Without oxygen, sewage is only partly broken down, leaving some harmful products.

4. Upgrading waste

Many manufacturing processes produce organic waste products. These can be fed to microbes which convert them to products which are useful to people and other animals. The advantage is that unwanted waste products are converted to products with a high energy and protein value. They also have a higher economic value than the original waste.

type of waste	useful product	use made of product
manure	biogas	fuel
fruit pulp	food rich in protein	animal feed

5. Fuels from microbes

When microbes grow on fresh manure, they produce methane gas. When yeast feeds on sugar, it produces alcohol. Both the methane and the alcohol can be used as fuels.

These two fuels are described as **renewable** energy sources whereas fossil fuels (coal, oil and gas) are **non-renewable** energy sources. There are advantages to using renewable energy sources rather than fossil fuels. They are harmless to the environment, easy and cheap to obtain, and will never be used up.

6. Other uses of microbes

Microbes can reproduce very rapidly by dividing into two. If they have food, water and heat, one bacterium can result in many hundreds of bacteria within a few hours. Industry makes use of fast growing bacteria to produce protein-rich foods, as a high percentage of a bacterium is protein.

Bacteria can be grown, harvested and dried to form a protein-rich powder called single-celled protein which is used as animal feed.

Some fungi produce a protein, called mycoprotein, which can be processed to produce meat-like products for cooking.

7. The carbon cycle

Decay is important in nature to ensure that minerals locked up in dead animals and plants are recycled. Both the nitrogen and carbon cycle involve bacteria. The carbon cycle involves the recycling of carbon.

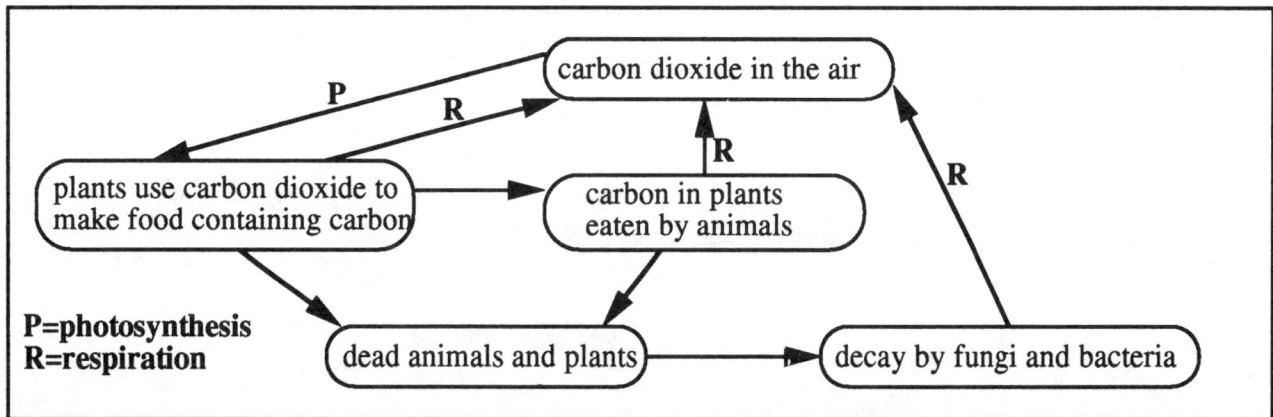

Reprogramming Microbes

1. Genetic engineering

Genetic engineering is a technique which involves taking a gene from one organism and transfering it into a bacterium. The bacterium then makes the chemical for which the transferred gene contains the information. As the bacterium reproduces rapidly, all the new bacteria will also make this chemical. In this way, large quantities of a chemical, such as insulin, can be made.

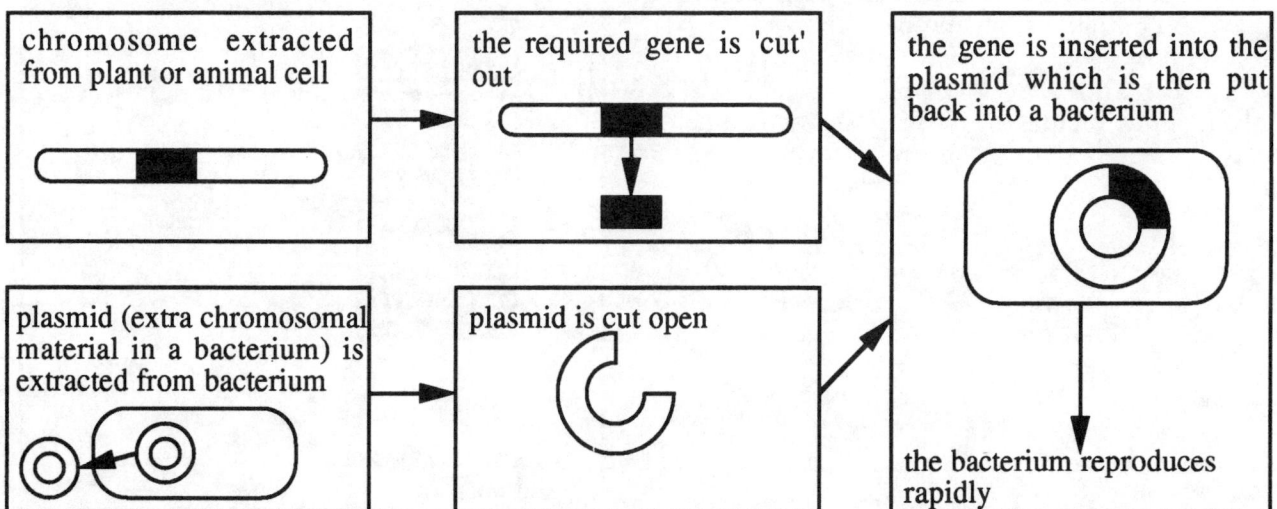

2. Products of genetic engineering

Insulin is a hormone produced in the pancreas and controls the blood sugar level. People who suffer from diabetes cannot make their own insulin. Until recently, sufferers used sheep and pig insulin but some people are allergic to it as it is not identical to human insulin. Genetic engineering can reprogramme bacteria to produce large amounts of insulin identical to human insulin. The gene which makes insulin can be cut from a human chromosome and inserted into a bacterial plasmid. The rapidly dividing bacteria produce the insulin which can be collected and purified. Genetic engineering and selective breeding both involve altering the genotype of an organism. Genetic engineering is faster and produces the organism with the new genotype immediately. Selective breeding is a long process which does not always produce the organism required.

3. Antibiotics

Other important products of genetic engineering are antibiotics, which can kill certain harmful bacteria. The most well known antibiotic is **penicillin**, which is produced by a fungus. There are many other antibiotics such as streptomycin and erythromycin. A single antibiotic is not always effective against bacteria, as many bacteria become resistant to a particular antibiotic, so new antibiotics are constantly being developed.

4. Biological detergents

Biological detergents contain enzymes produced by bacteria. These are able to breakdown difficult protein stains such as grass, blood and egg. Biological detergents are effective at removing stains at low temperatures (40°C) which non-biological detergents would not remove. Stain removal at such low temperatures prevents damage being done to fabrics and saves on fuel costs.

5. Immobilisation

Immobilisation is a technique that fixes enzymes onto substances such as jelly or glass beads so that they can be used again and again without having to separate them continually from the product of their action. Whole cells, such as yeast, can be immobilised in this way.

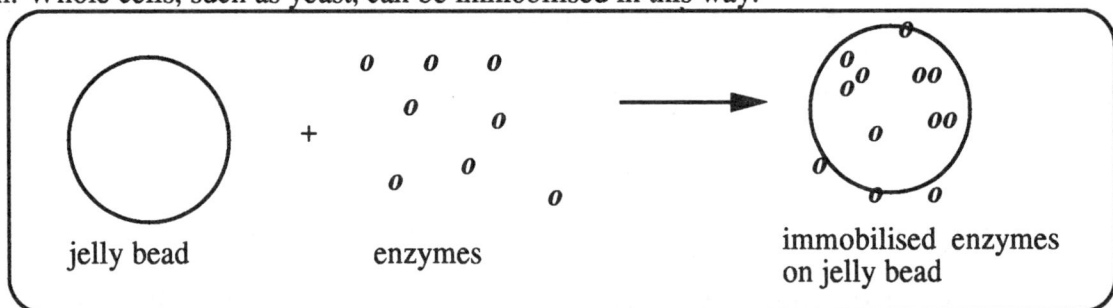

jelly bead   enzymes   immobilised enzymes
                                     on jelly bead

6. Continuous flow processing

Immobilised enzymes are placed in a fermenter. Nutrients can be continually fed in and the end products continuously collected and purified. This is known as continuous flow processing.

This method increases productivity and reduces costs compared with batch processing as used in brewing.

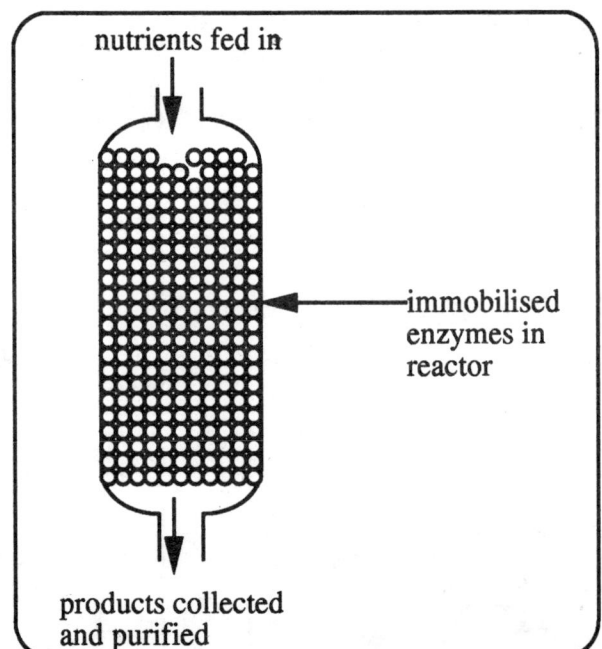

nutrients fed in

immobilised enzymes in reactor

products collected and purified